Sing at First Sight...
More Melodies!

REPRODUCIBLE EXERCISES FOR SIGHT-SINGING PRACTICE

Andy Beck • Brian Lewis

MW00851574

How to Use This Book

Designed to be used in conjunction with *Sing at First Sight (Levels 1 & 2)* and the *Reproducible Companion* book/CDs, *More Melodies!* provides reinforcement and learning extensions for the concepts introduced throughout this complete sight-singing course.

Rhythm Readiness pages at the beginning of each unit are designed to be spoken, clapped, tapped, or sung on a pitch.

Sequential Pitch Exercises are designed to challenge, yet nurture developing sight-singers. There are many excellent techniques that work well with sight-singing. It is recommended that students sing the exercises in this book using solfège syllables to help establish a tonal base. However, it is not the intention of the authors to require the use of any single methodology, but rather to provide tools to allow teachers to make instructional choices that fit their own personal teaching style.

Challenge Exercises, included in each lesson, are slightly more difficult. In addition to regular practice, they may be used for exams, friendly classroom competitions, or extra credit work.

How to Use This CD

Reproducible PDF files of each lesson are included on the enclosed disc. The purchase of this CD carries with it the right to display these images on an interactive whiteboard and/or post them on a website. Limited to one school/organization only.

Table of Contents

Alfred Music
P.O. Box 10003
Van Nuys, CA 91410-0003
alfred.com

ISBN-10: 1-4706-1562-2
ISBN-13: 978-1-4706-1562-8

$\frac{4}{4}$ Time, C Major, F Major, Quarter Note, Quarter Rest, Do, Re, Half Note, Half Rest, Mi, Fa, Whole Note, Whole Rest, Sol, La, Eighth Note, Eighth Rest, Ti, High Do

Rhythm Readiness 1

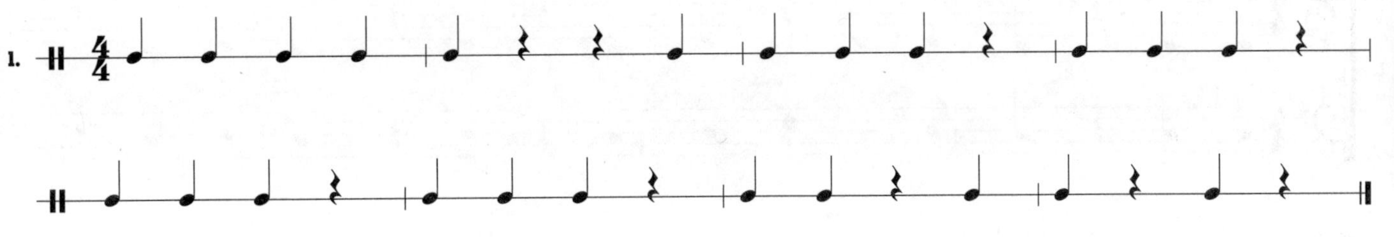

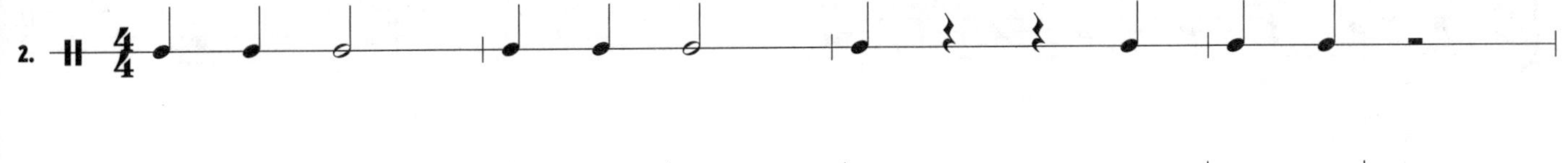

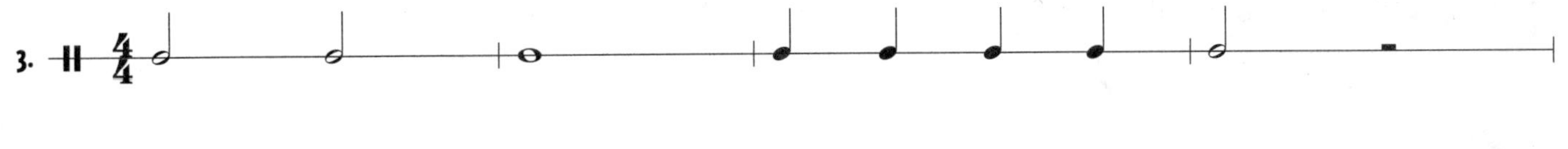

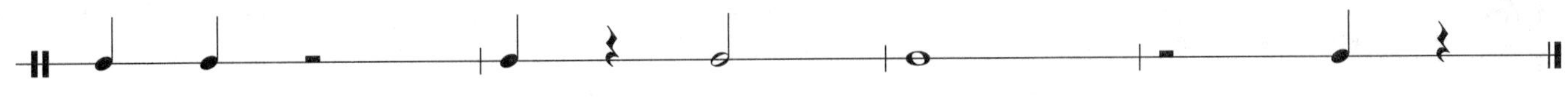

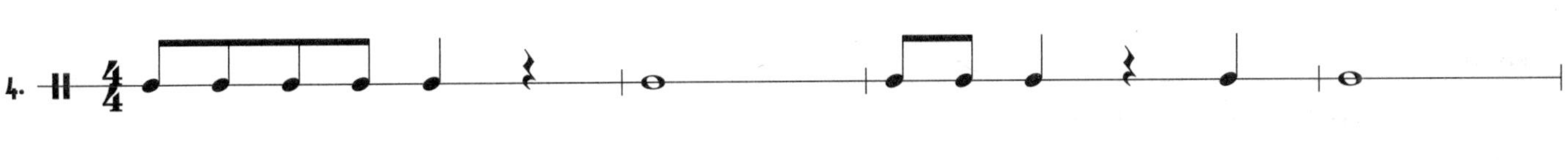

Challenge Exercise

Lesson 1

The following exercises correspond with Lesson 1 in the *Sing at First Sight, Level 1* Textbook and Reproducible Companion.

Hint

Be sure to keep a steady pulse, even during the rests.

4.
5.
Challenge Exercise
6.

Lesson 2

The following exercises correspond with Lesson 2 in the *Sing at First Sight, Level 1* Textbook and Reproducible Companion.

1.

2.

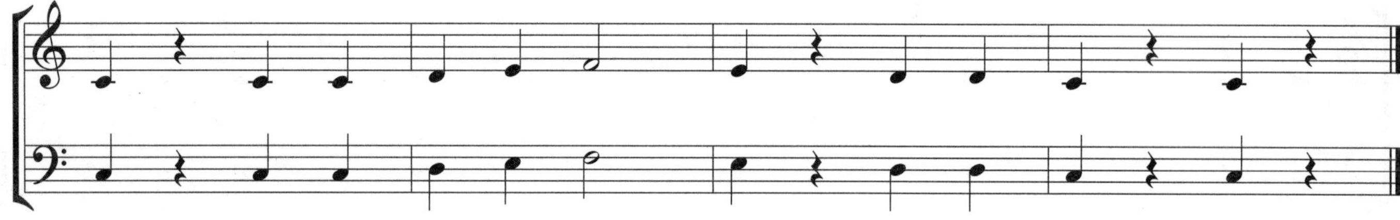

Hint

Before you sing, identify the key signature and locations of *Do*.

3.

4.
Challenge Exercise
5.
6.

Lesson 3

The following exercises correspond with Lesson 3 in the *Sing at First Sight, Level 1* Textbook and Reproducible Companion.

Hint

Concentrate during long rests, attempting to internalize the next pitch during the silence.

4.

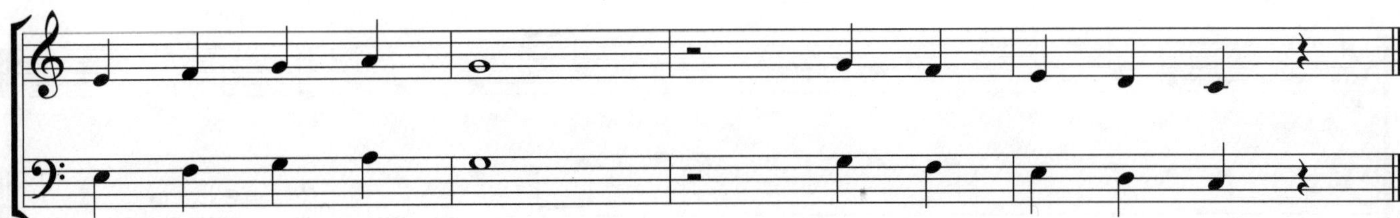

Challenge Exercise

5.

6.

Lesson 4

The following exercises correspond with Lesson 4 in the *Sing at First Sight, Level 1* Textbook and Reproducible Companion.

Hint

It's very important to subdivide the beats as you sight-sing.

4.

5.

Challenge Exercise

6.

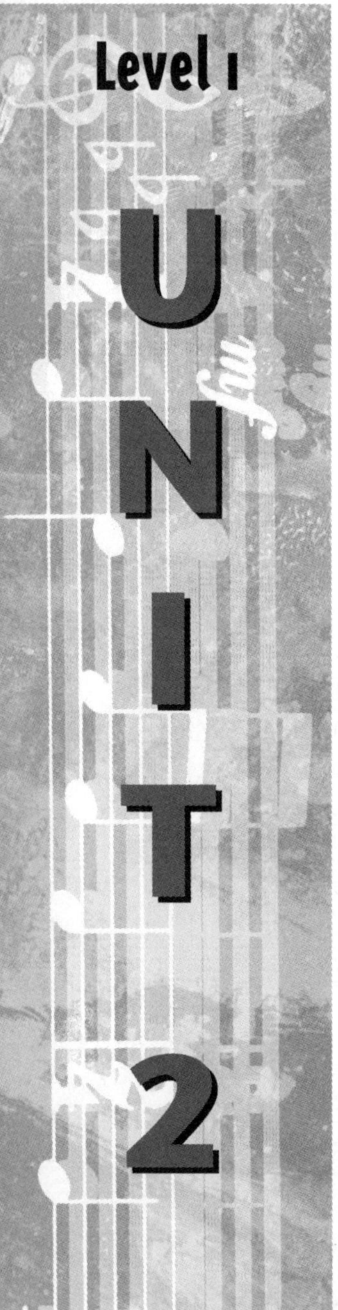

Repeat Sign, 1st and 2nd Endings, G Major, D Major, Tie, Dotted Half Note, Low Ti, High Re, Dotted Quarter Note, Low La, Low Sol, Intervals, 2nds, 3rds

Rhythm Readiness 2

1.

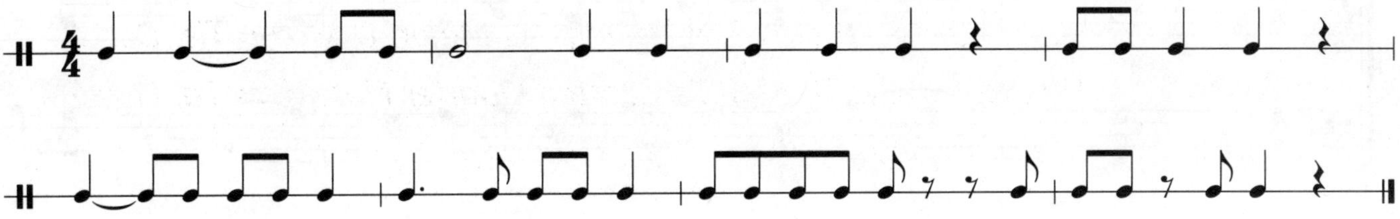

2.

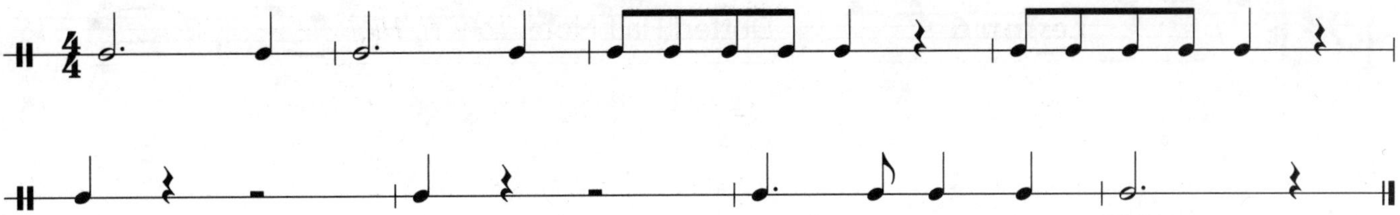

3.

1.

2.

Challenge Exercise

Lesson 5

The following exercises correspond with Lesson 5 in the *Sing at First Sight, Level 1* Textbook and Reproducible Companion.

1.

2.

Challenge Exercise

3.

4.

Hint

Carefully follow the contour of the melodic line, moving up and down or staying the same when appropriate.

5.

6.

Lesson 6

The following exercises correspond with Lesson 6 in the *Sing at First Sight, Level 1* Textbook and Reproducible Companion.

4.

Hint

Sustain longer notes for their full duration and release shorter ones as indicated by the rests.

5.

6.

Lesson 7

The following exercises correspond with Lesson 7 in the *Sing at First Sight, Level 1* Textbook and Reproducible Companion.

1.

Hint

Before singing this exercise, determine which rhythms fall directly on the beats and which fall on the offbeats.

2.

3.

1.

2.

After singing exercises 4 and 5 separately, perform them simultaneously!

4.

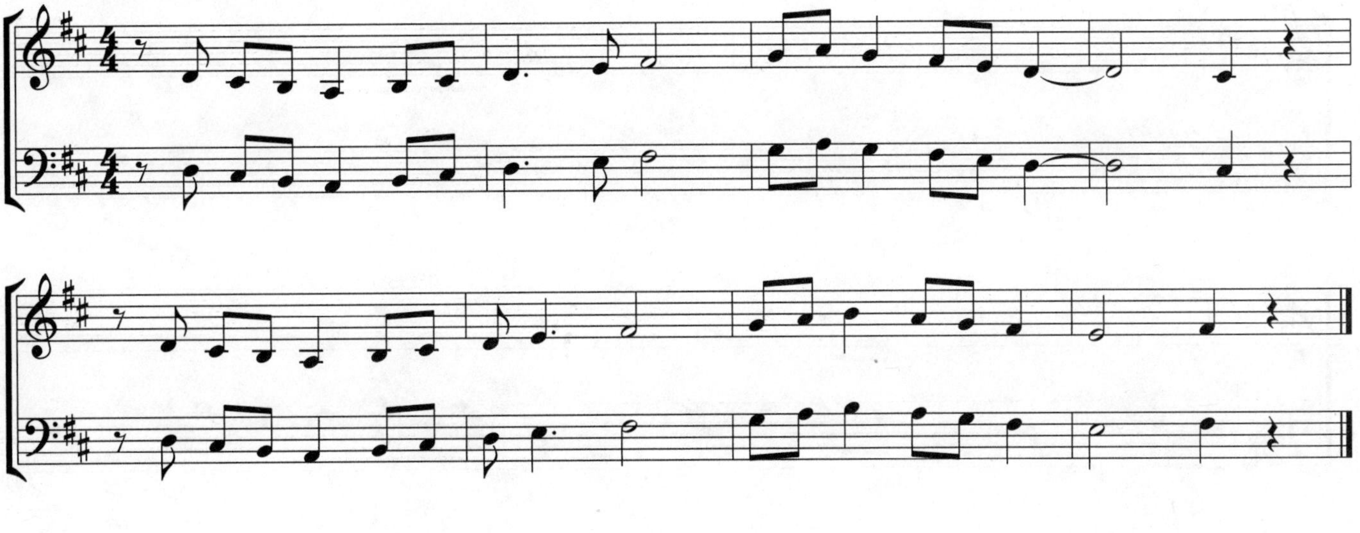

5.

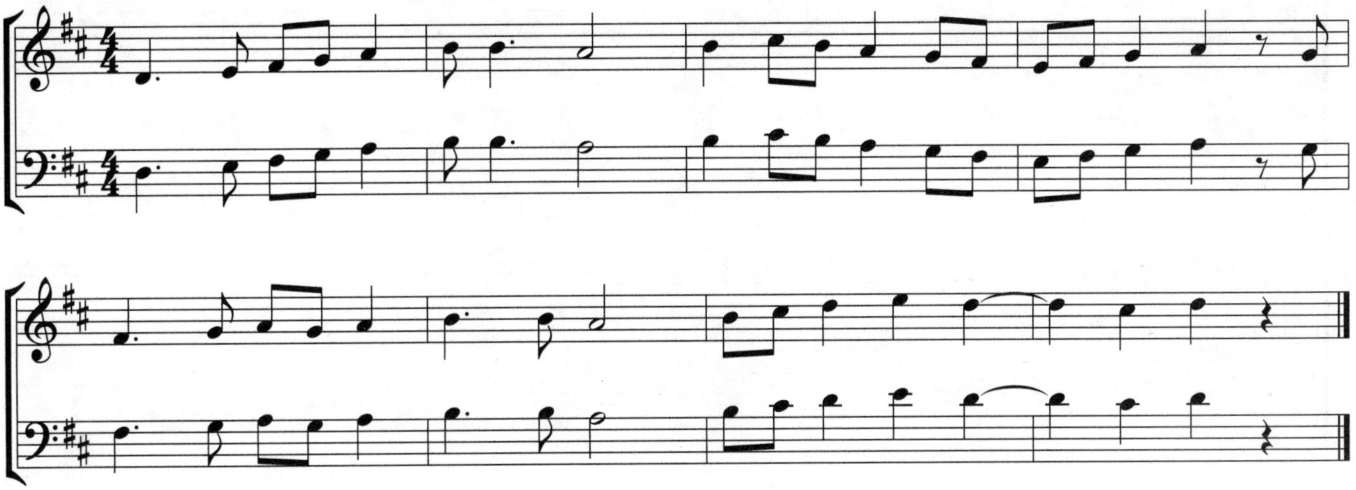

6.

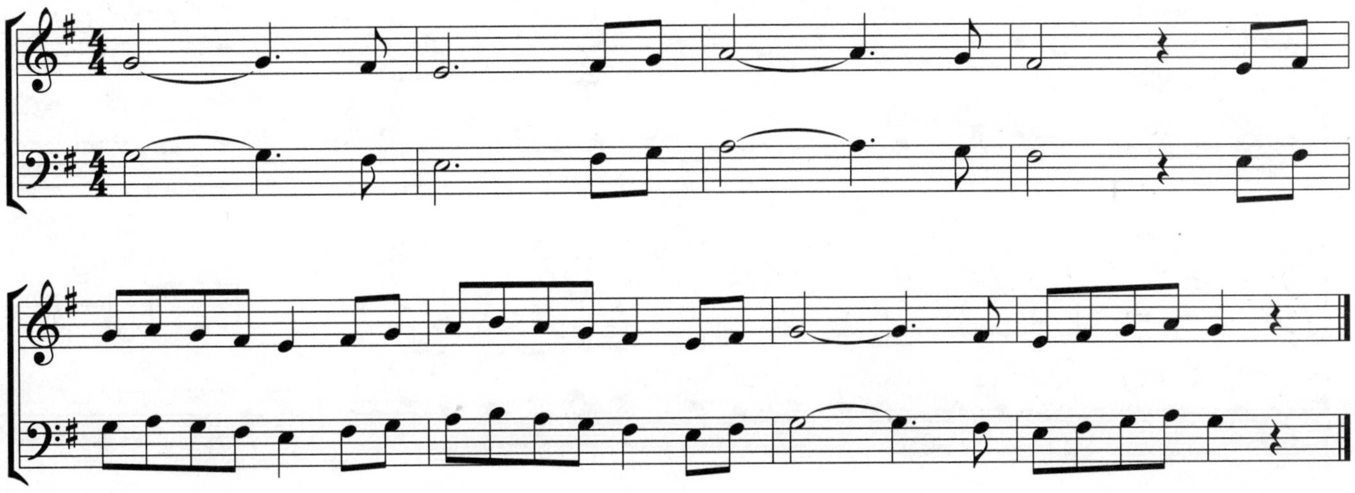

Lesson 8

The following exercises correspond with Lesson 8 in the *Sing at First Sight, Level 1* Textbook and Reproducible Companion.

1.

2.

1.

2.

Hint

It is very helpful to remember recently sung pitches in order to find upcoming notes.

3.

Challenge Exercise

This tune can be performed as a two-part round. Part 2 begins when Part 1 gets to the fifth measure.

*Dynamic Signs (**pp**, **p**, **mp**, **mf**, **f**, **ff**), Crescendo, Decrescendo, B♭ Major, E♭ Major, $\frac{3}{4}$ Time, $\frac{2}{4}$ Time, 8ths/Octaves, Eighth-Quarter-Eighth Note Pattern, 4ths, 5ths*

Rhythm Readiness 3

1.
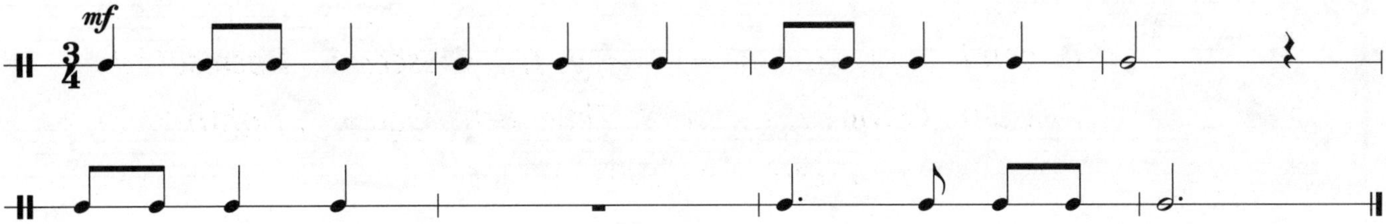
mf

2.
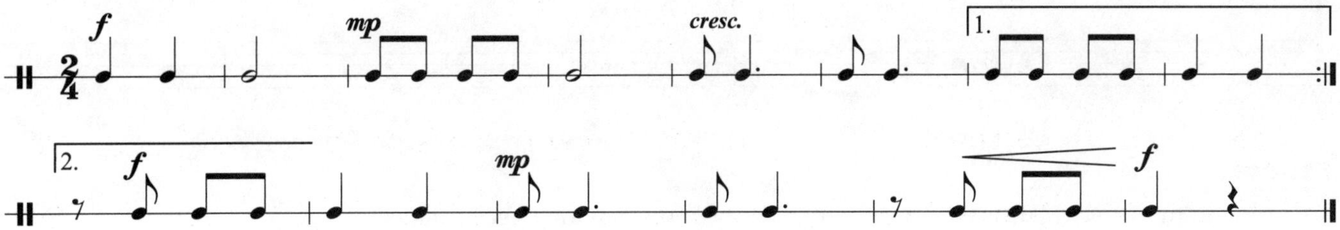
f
mp
cresc.
1.
2.
f
mp
f

3.
mf

Challenge Exercise

4.
f
p
f
1.
2.
pp

5.
mf
mp
cresc.
ff

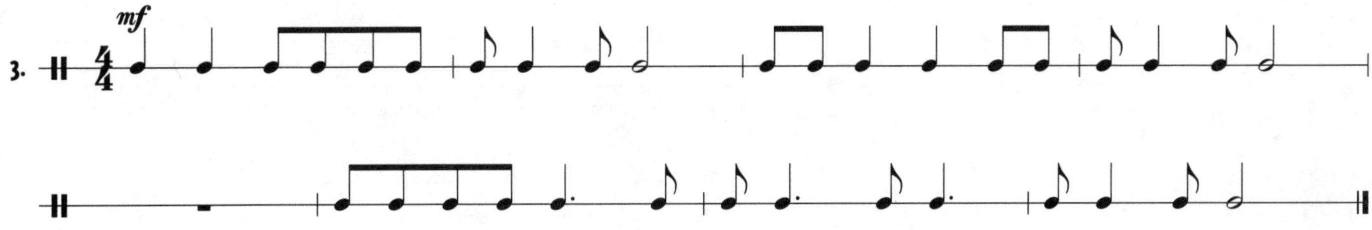

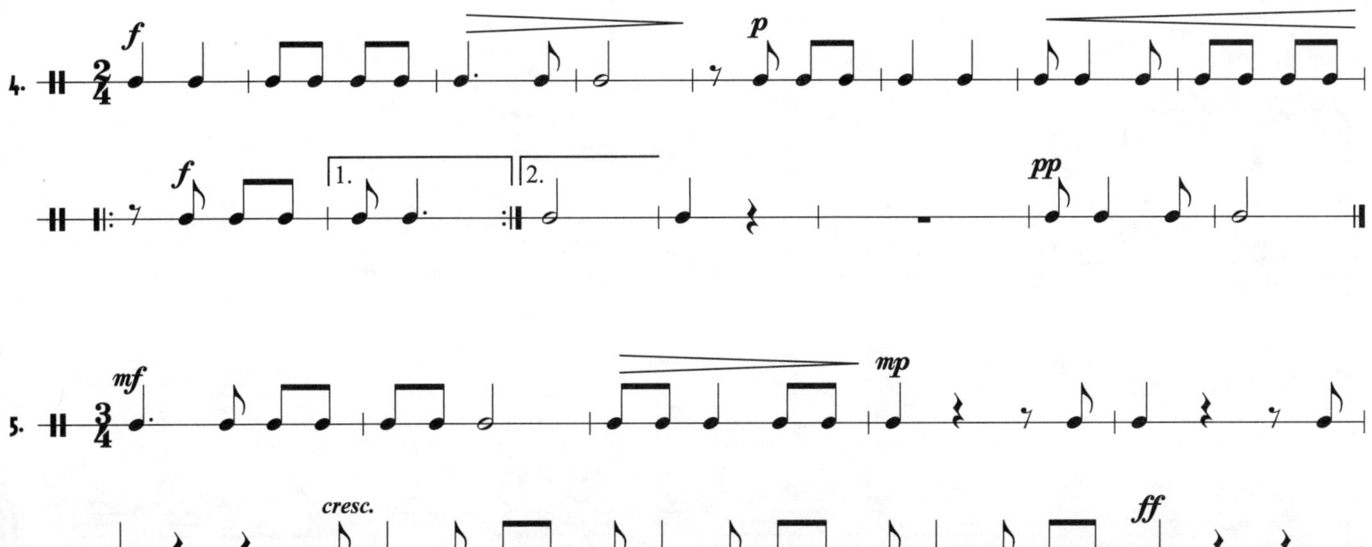

Lesson 9

The following exercises correspond with Lesson 9 in the *Sing at First Sight, Level 1* Textbook and Reproducible Companion.

Hint

Observing marked dynamics will always enhance the musicality of a performance.

2.

3.

LEVEL 1 • UNIT 3

Lesson 10

The following exercises correspond with Lesson 10 in the *Sing at First Sight, Level 1* Textbook and Reproducible Companion.

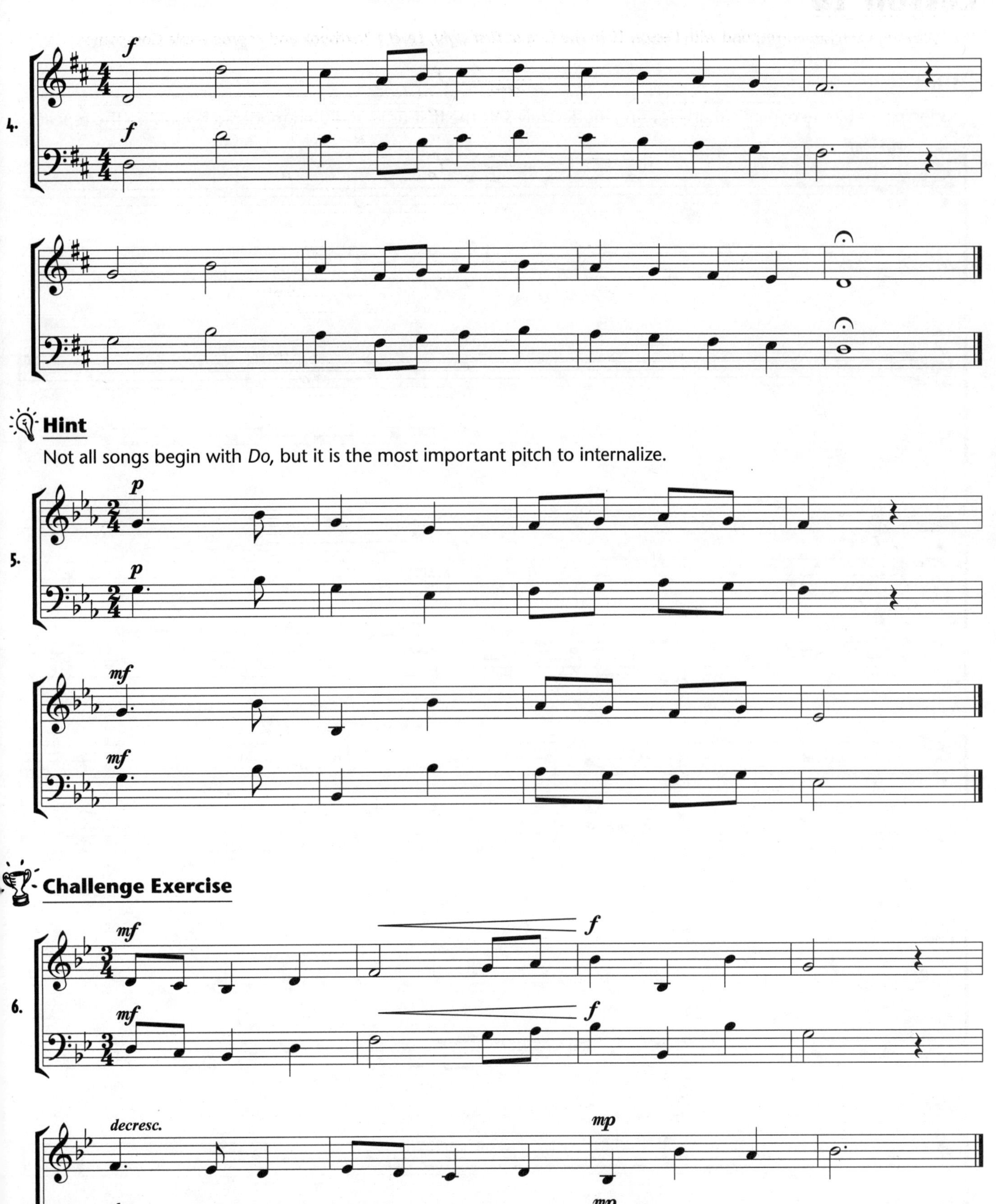
f
4.
f
Hint
Not all songs begin with Do, but it is the most important pitch to internalize.
p
5.
p
mf
mf
Challenge Exercise
mf
f
6.
mf
f
decresc.
mp
decresc.
mp

Lesson 11

The following exercises correspond with Lesson 11 in the *Sing at First Sight, Level 1* Textbook and Reproducible Companion.

Hint

As indicated by the dynamic marking, sing moderately soft the first time and then moderately loud on the repeat.

LEVEL 1 • UNIT 3

Challenge Exercise

Lesson 12

The following exercises correspond with Lesson 12 in the *Sing at First Sight, Level 1* Textbook and Reproducible Companion.

4.

mf

mf

p

p

LEVEL 1 • UNIT 3

5.

mf

mf

Hint

Do and *Sol* are the most important reference points.
Use your eyes to recognize their position on the staff and your ears to remember their sound within the key.

6.

f

f

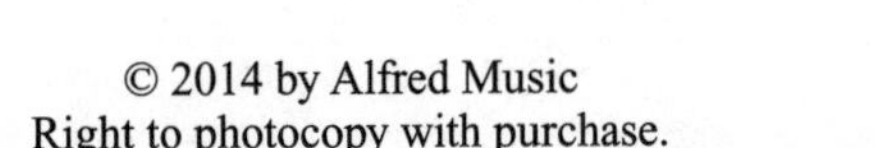

Da Capo, Dal Segno, Fine, Coda, A Major, E Major, 6ths, 7ths, Changing Meter, Pick-up Notes, Sixteenth Notes, Sixteenth-Eighth Note Patterns

Rhythm Readiness 4

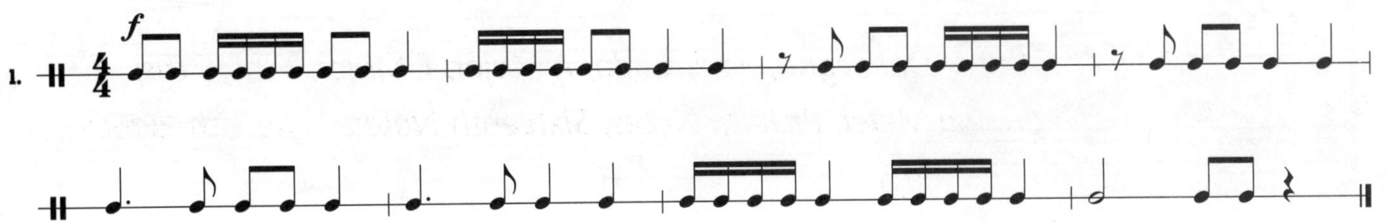

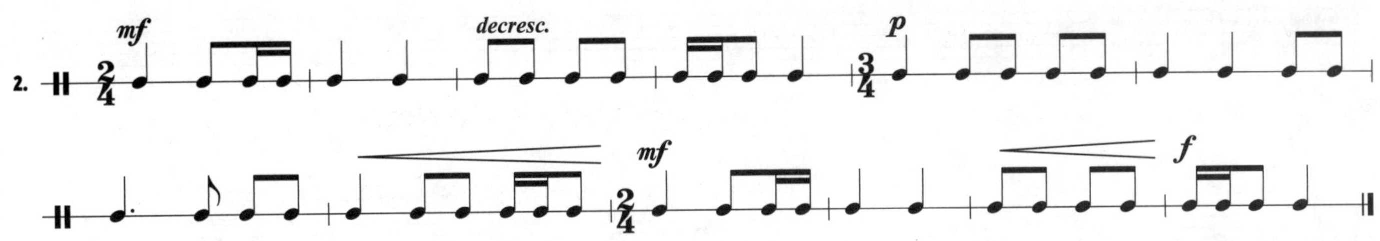

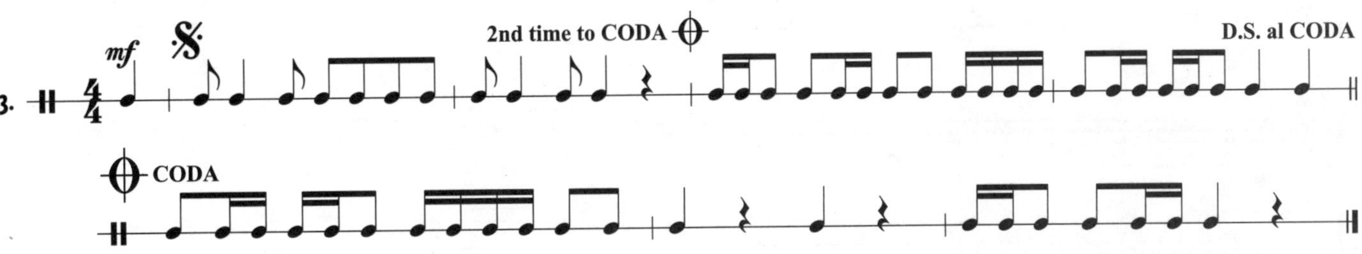

Challenge Exercise

Lesson 13

The following exercises correspond with Lesson 13 in the *Sing at First Sight, Level 1* Textbook and Reproducible Companion.

Challenge Exercise

LEVEL 1 • UNIT 4

Lesson 14

The following exercises correspond with Lesson 14 in the *Sing at First Sight, Level 1* Textbook and Reproducible Companion.

Hint

Before singing an exercise, take a moment of silent study to identify challenging intervals and rhythms.

2.

f

mp

f

3.

pp - f

mf

1.

2.

Challenge Exercise

Lesson 15

The following exercises correspond with Lesson 15 in the *Sing at First Sight, Level 1* Textbook and Reproducible Companion.

1.

mp
cresc.
mp
cresc.
mf
f
mf
f

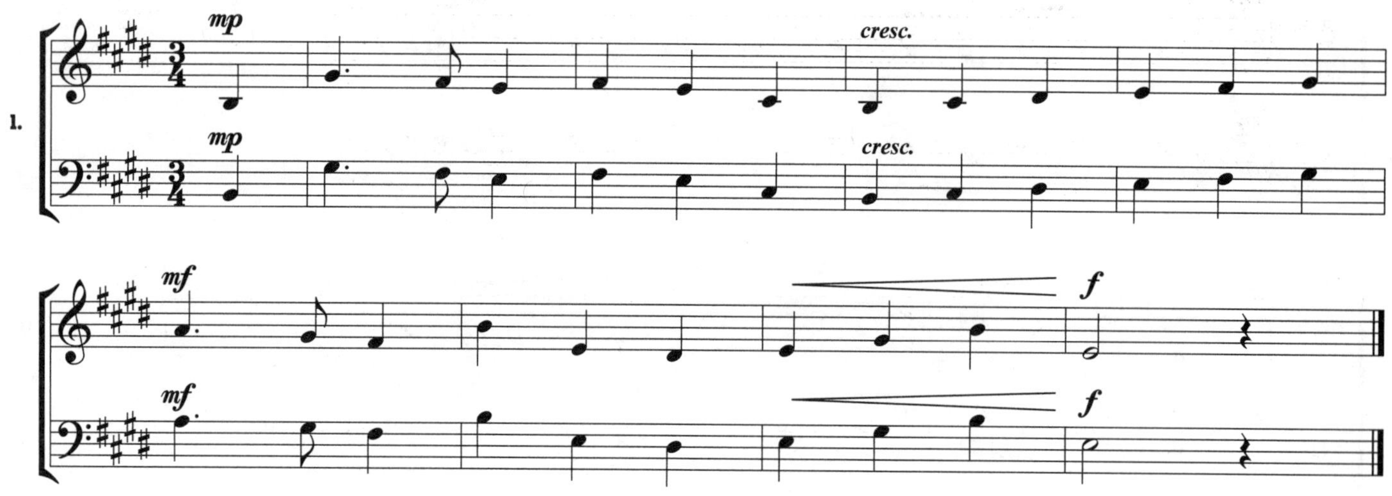

Hint

Look for patterns (both melodic and rhythmic).

2.

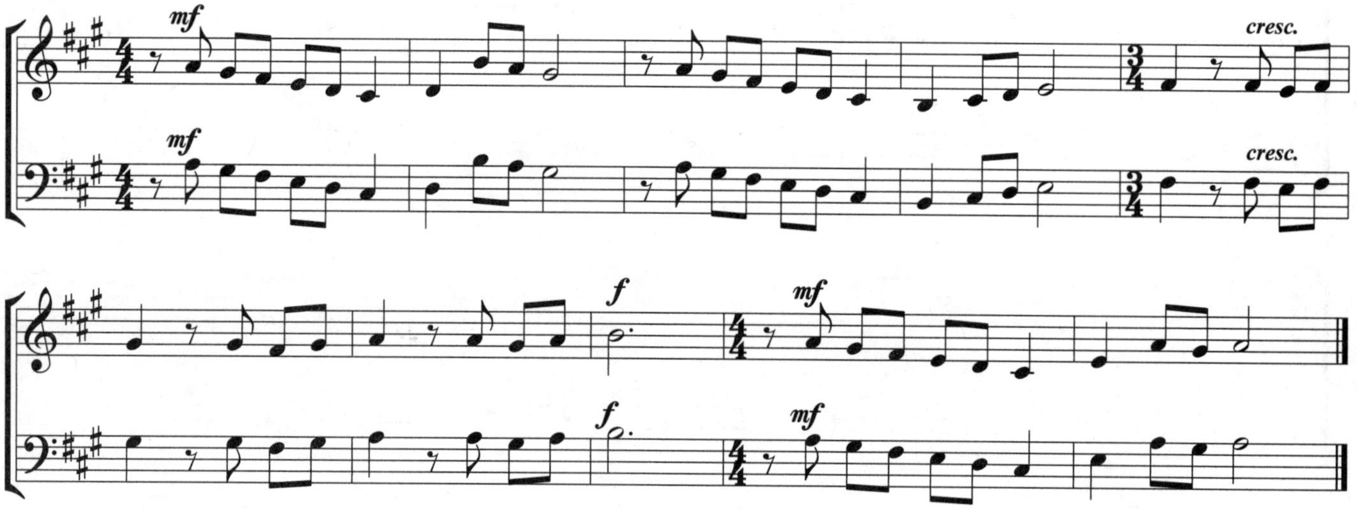
mf
cresc.
mf
cresc.
f
mf
f
mf

3.

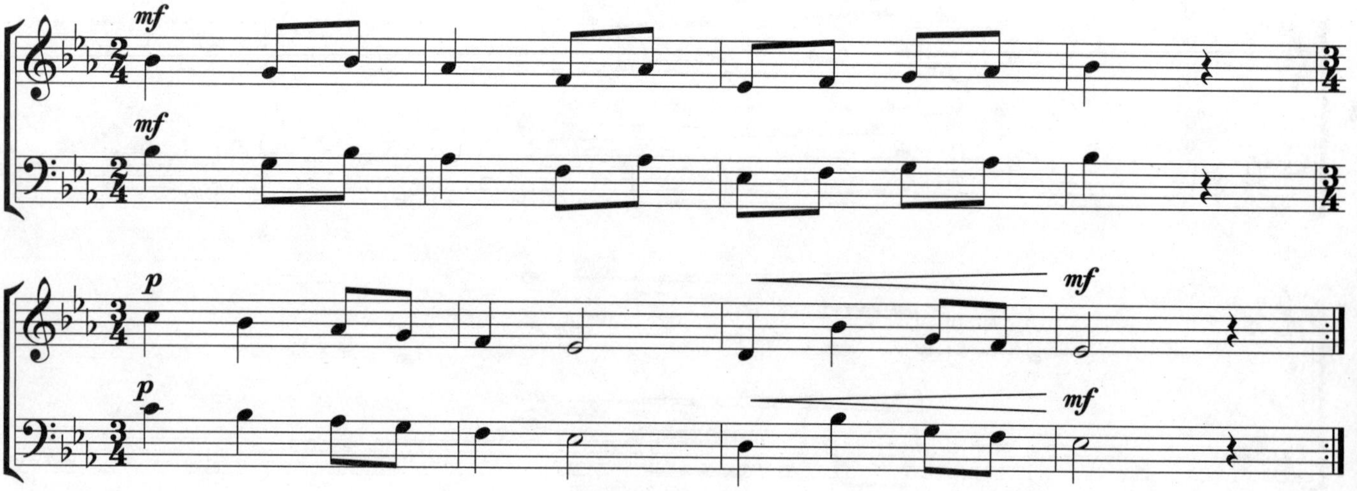
mf
mf
p
mf
p
mf

LEVEL 1 • UNIT 4

Lesson 16

The following exercises correspond with Lesson 16 in the *Sing at First Sight, Level 1* Textbook and Reproducible Companion.

Hint

At this level, it will be helpful to subdivide sixteenth notes throughout (1 e & a, 2 e & a, etc.)

LEVEL 1 • UNIT 4

Challenge Exercise

6.

mf

mf

1.

2.

Articulation Marks (Slur/Legato, Staccato, Marcato/Accent, Tenuto), A♭ Major, D♭ Major, Rounds/Canons, Two-Part Harmony, Dotted Eighth Note, Dotted Eighth-Sixteenth Note Patterns, Triplet

Rhythm Readiness 5

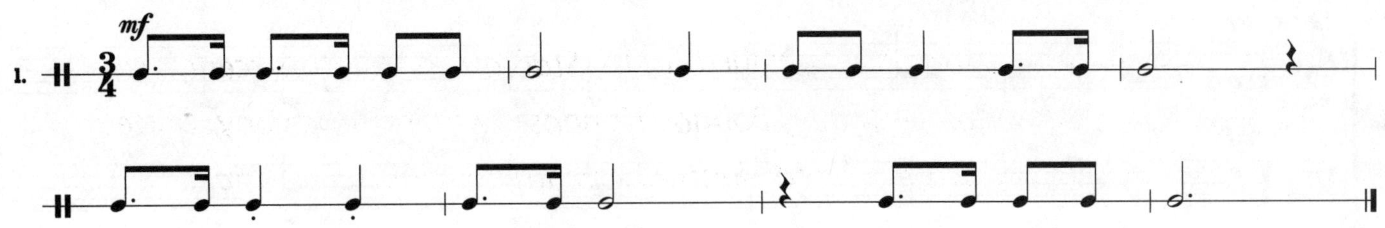

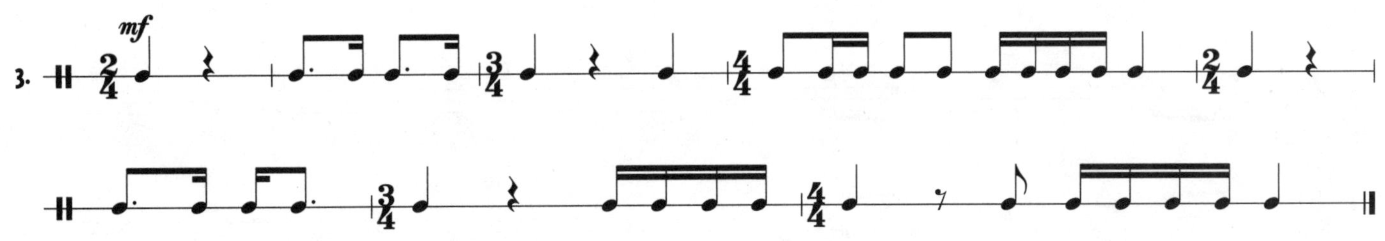

Challenge Exercise

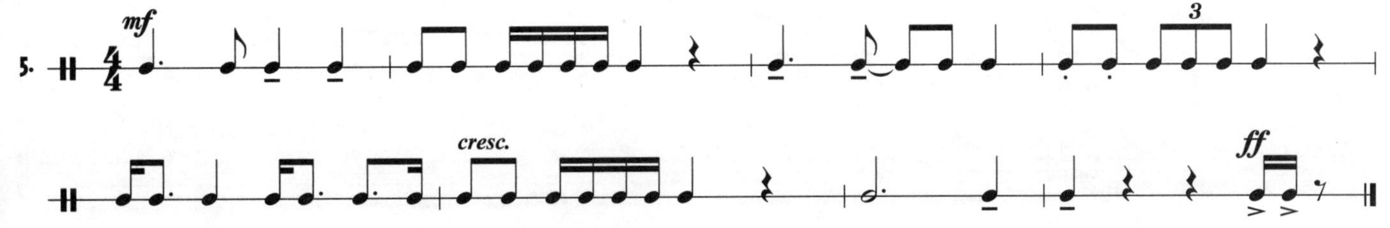

Lesson 17

The following exercises correspond with Lesson 17 in the *Sing at First Sight, Level 1* Textbook and Reproducible Companion. All of the exercises in this lesson can be performed in canon.

Hint

To achieve the best *staccato*, shorten the note by half and attack with a slight emphasis.

2.

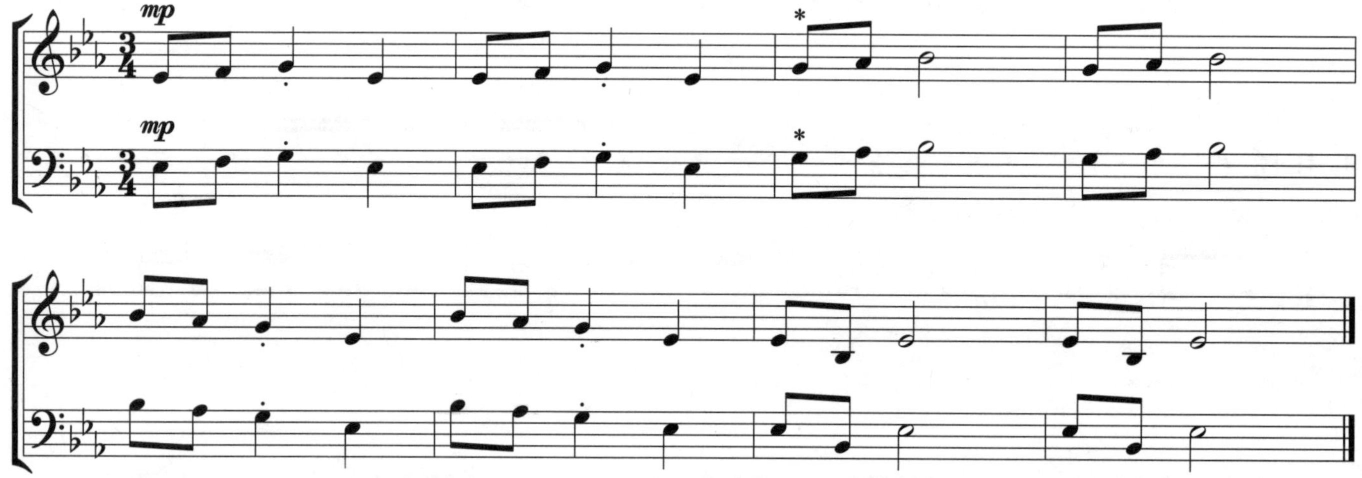

mp

3.

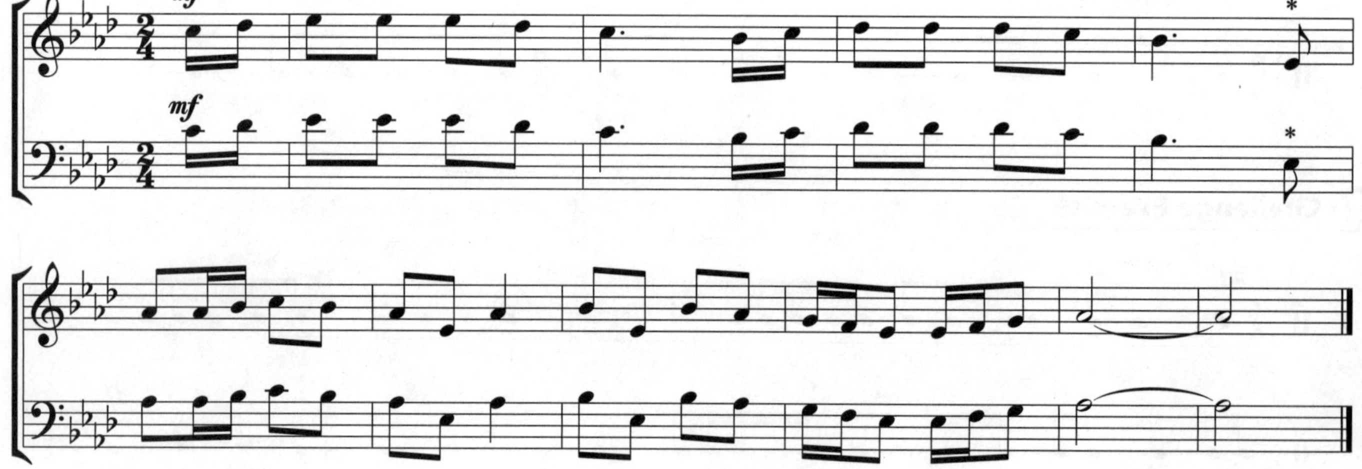

mf

4.
p
p
5.
f
f
Challenge Exercise
6.
mp
mf
mp

Lesson 18

The following exercises correspond with Lesson 18 in the *Sing at First Sight, Level 1* Textbook and Reproducible Companion.

1.

2.

Hint

When all voices sing the same pitch in the same octave, it is called *perfect prime* or *perfect unison*. Be sure to match and tune those notes as you perform.

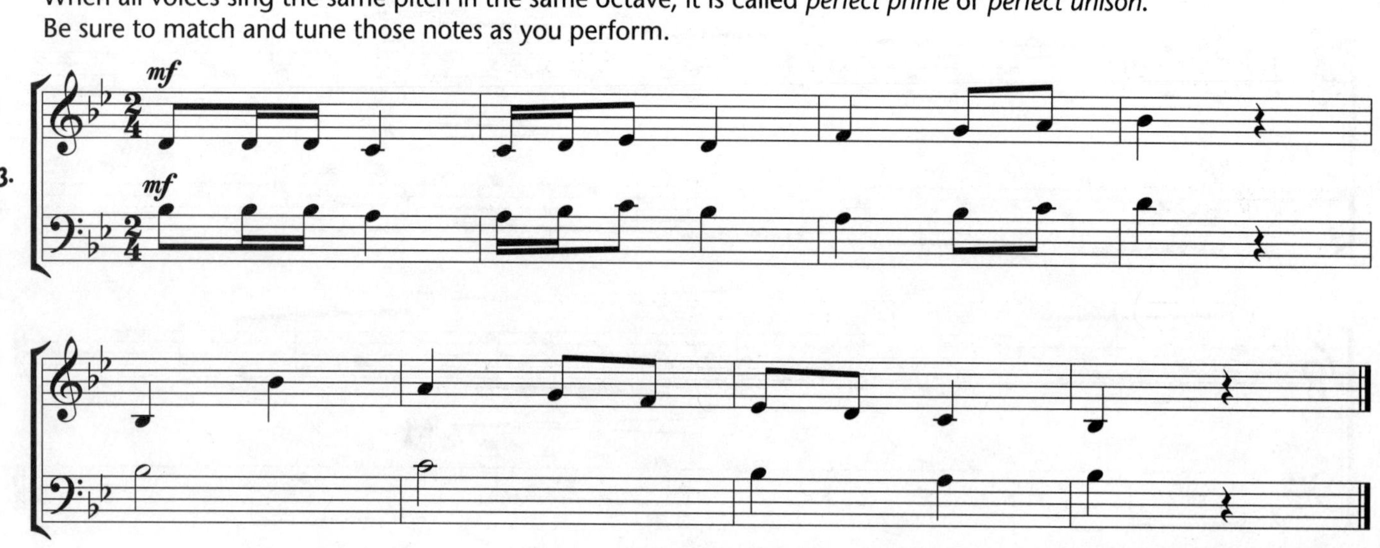

4.
mf
f
5.
f - p
Challenge Exercise
6.
mp
mf
1.
2.
rit.
p

Lesson 19

The following exercises correspond with Lesson 19 in the *Sing at First Sight, Level 1* Textbook and Reproducible Companion.

1.

Hint

Notes that are marked with a slur should be sung especially connected, but not slowing in tempo.

2.

3.

4.
mp
p
1.
2.
pp
5.
f
cresc.
Challenge Exercise
6.
mf
p
LEVEL 1 • UNIT 5

Lesson 20

The following exercises correspond with Lesson 20 in the *Sing at First Sight, Level 1* Textbook and Reproducible Companion.

 **Hint**

Differentiate between beats that are divided into three equal parts and beats that are divided into four.

1.

2.

3.

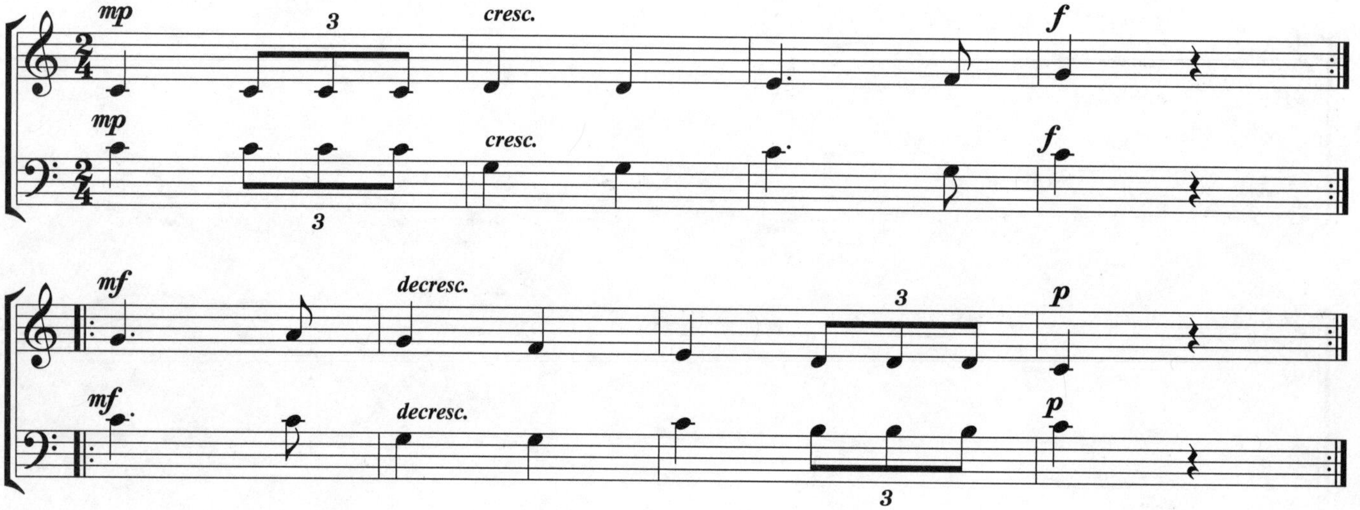

4.
mp
3
cresc.
mp cresc.
f
5.
mf
6.
pp
Challenge Exercise

Tempo Markings (Largo, Adagio, Andante, Moderato, Allegro, Presto, Ritardando/Rallentando, Accelerando, Molto, Poco a Poco), B Major, G♭ Major, $\frac{2}{2}$ Time/Cut Time, $\frac{6}{8}$ Time, $\frac{9}{8}$ Time, Three-Part Harmony

Rhythm Readiness 6

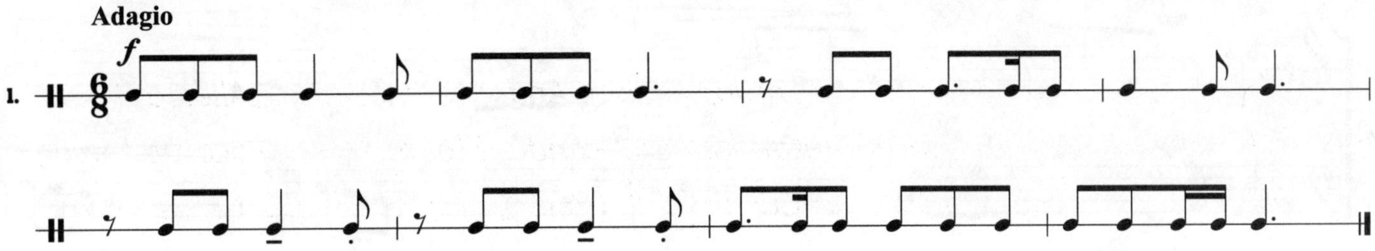
Adagio
f
1.
6/8

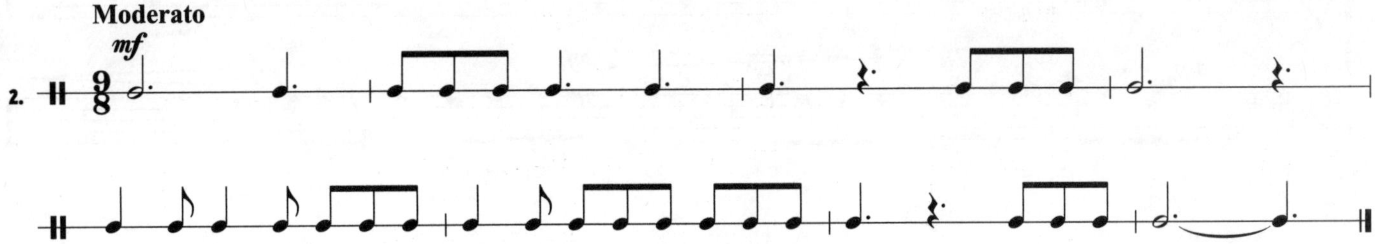
Moderato
mf
2.
9/8

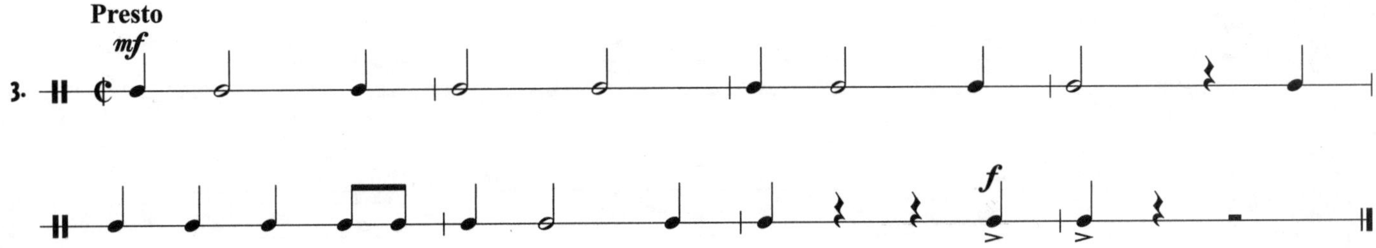
Presto
mf
3.
f

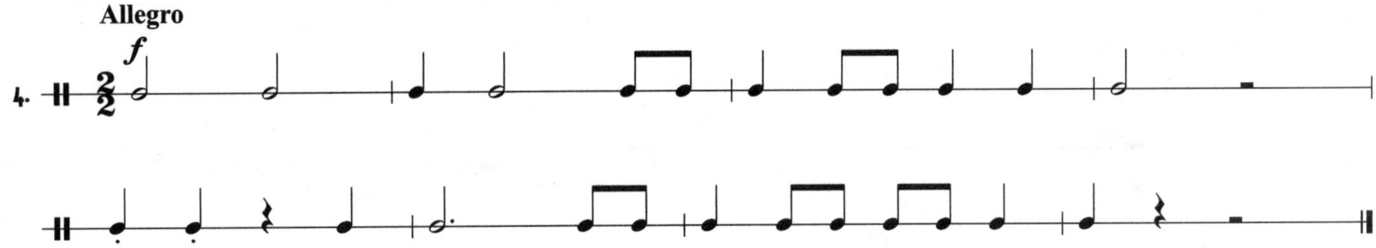
Allegro
f
4.
2/2

Challenge Exercise

Andante
mp
5.
9/8
6/8
cresc.
f

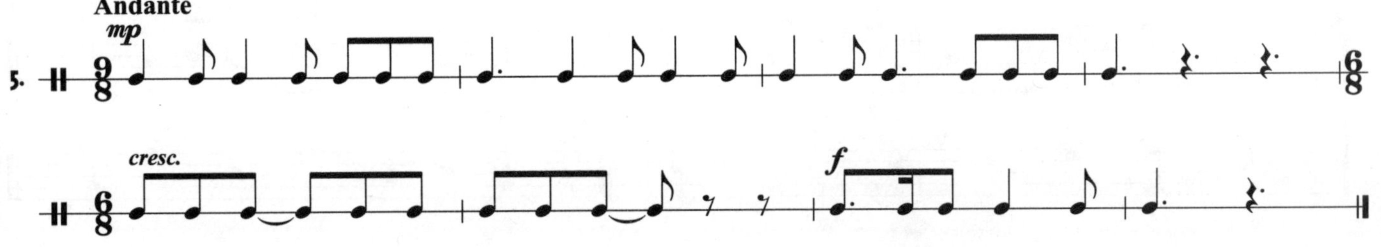

Lesson 21

The following exercises correspond with Lesson 21 in the *Sing at First Sight, Level 1* Textbook and Reproducible Companion.

Hint

It may be helpful to practice this $\frac{2}{2}$ exercise in $\frac{4}{4}$ at first.

Challenge Exercise

LEVEL 1 • UNIT 6

Lesson 22

The following exercises correspond with Lesson 22 in the *Sing at First Sight, Level 1* Textbook and Reproducible Companion.

1.
mf
mf

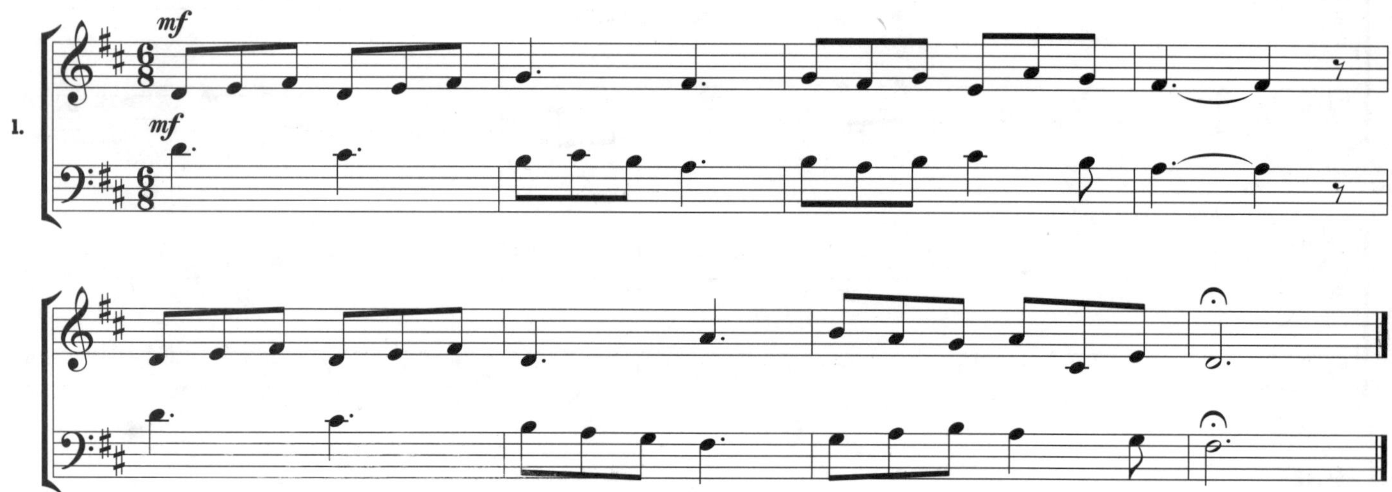

Hint

The accented notes should be performed *marcato*, with a firm stress.

2.
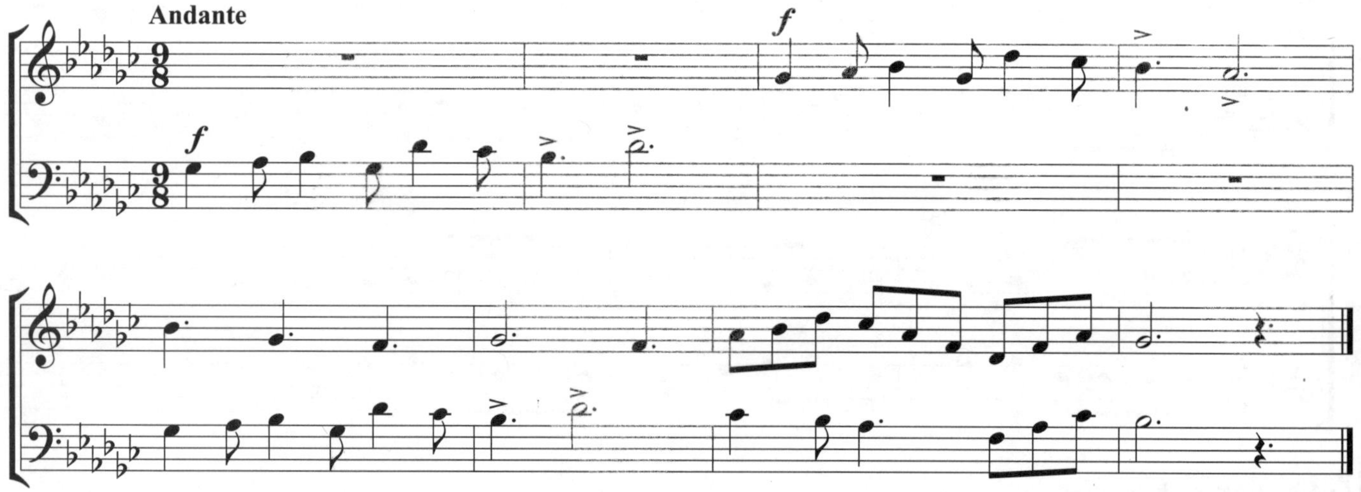
Andante
f
f

3.
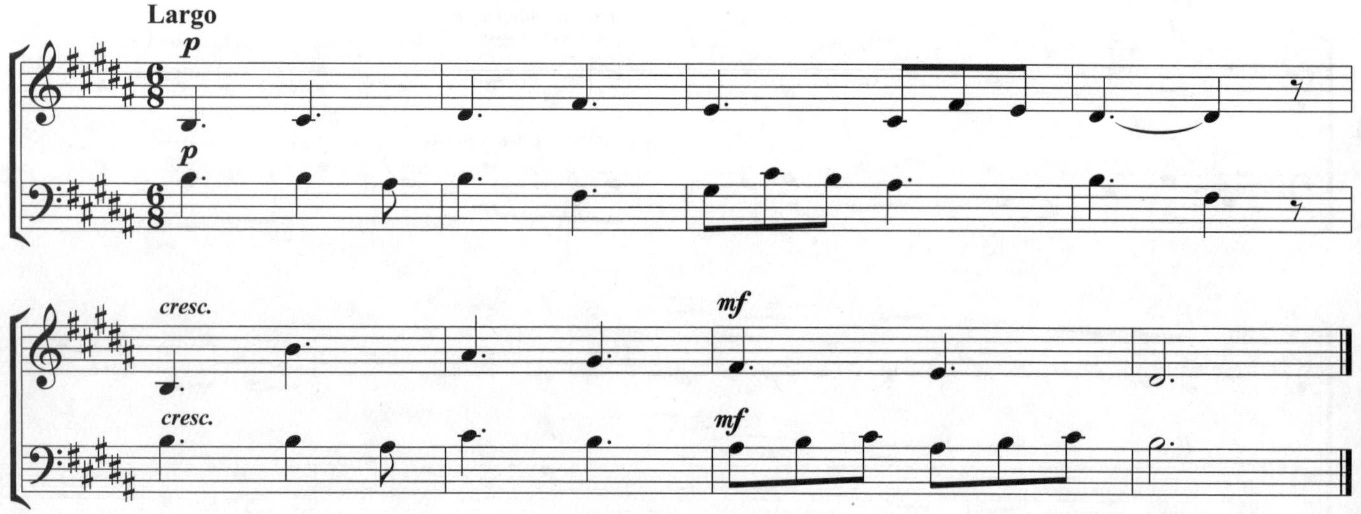
Largo
p
p
cresc.
mf
cresc.
mf

Moderato

4.

Presto

poco rall.

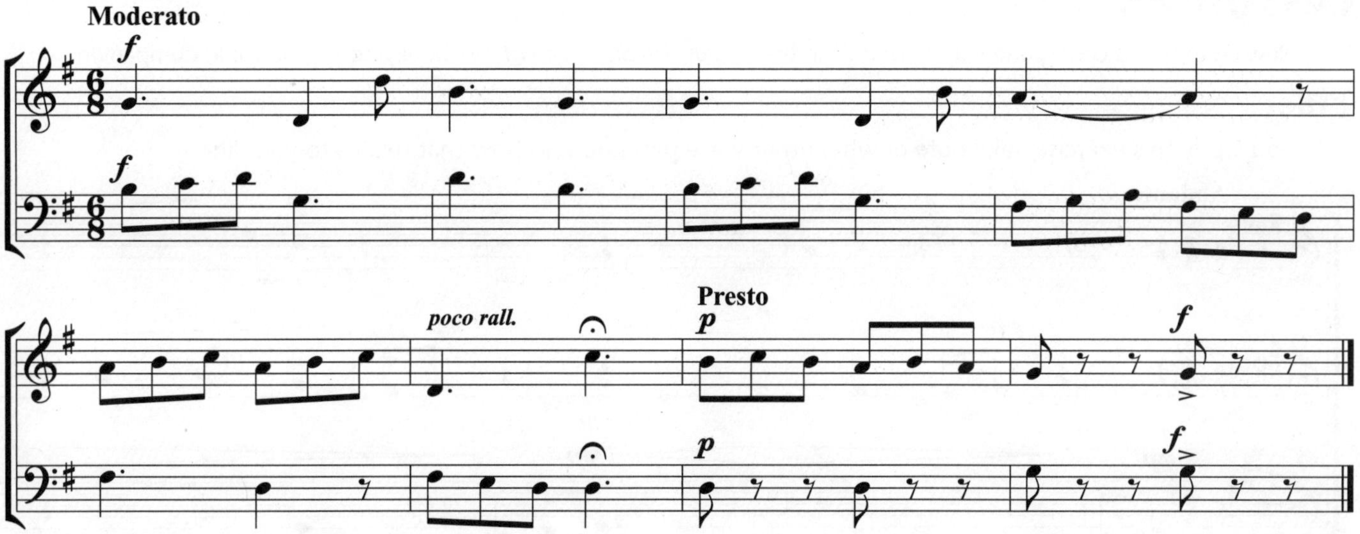

5.

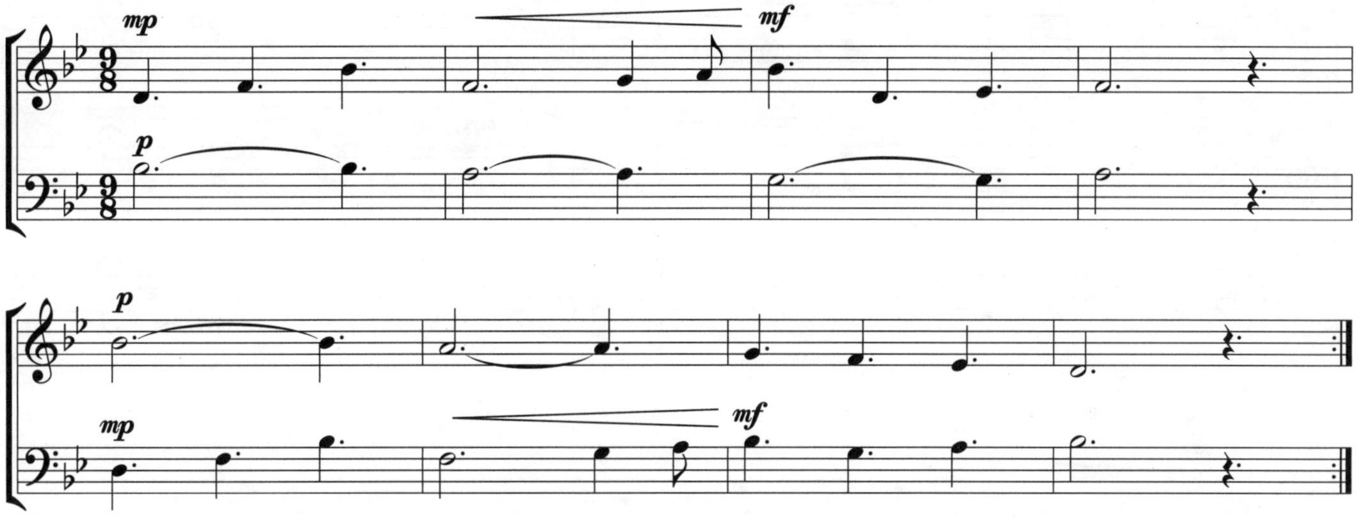

Challenge Exercise

Be sure to keep the eighth notes steady from measure to measure, meter to meter.

6.

Lesson 23

The following exercises correspond with Lesson 23 in the *Sing at First Sight, Level 1* Textbook and Reproducible Companion.

Hint

As you study this exercise, take note of what other voice parts do and how that relates to your line.

Moderato
3.
f
mp
Challenge Exercise
Largo
4.
mf
p
cresc.
f

Lesson 24

The following exercises correspond with Lesson 24 in the *Sing at First Sight, Level 1* Textbook and Reproducible Companion.

Hint

Perform with the indicated articulation to create musical contrast and interest.

Moderato

mp

3.

mp

Challenge Exercise

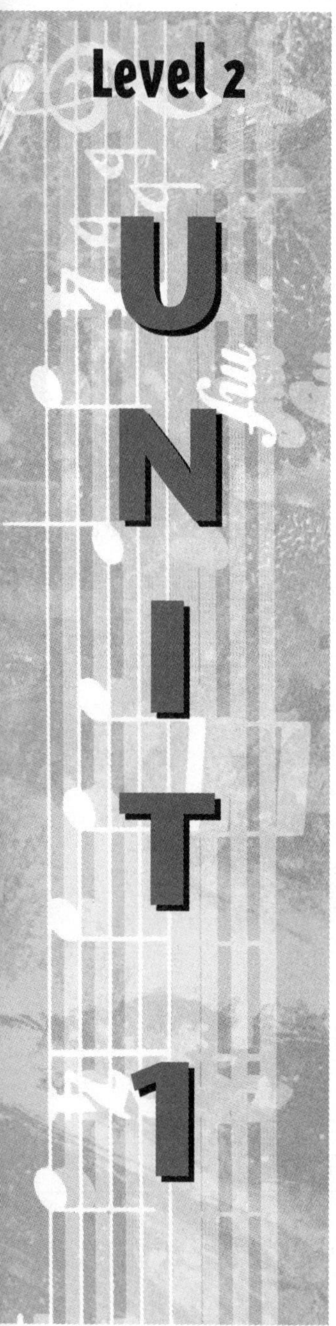

A Minor, D Minor, E Minor, Half and Whole Steps, Accidentals, Singing in Minor: La, Ti, Do, Re, Mi, Fa, Sol, High La, Fi, Si

Rhythm Readiness 7

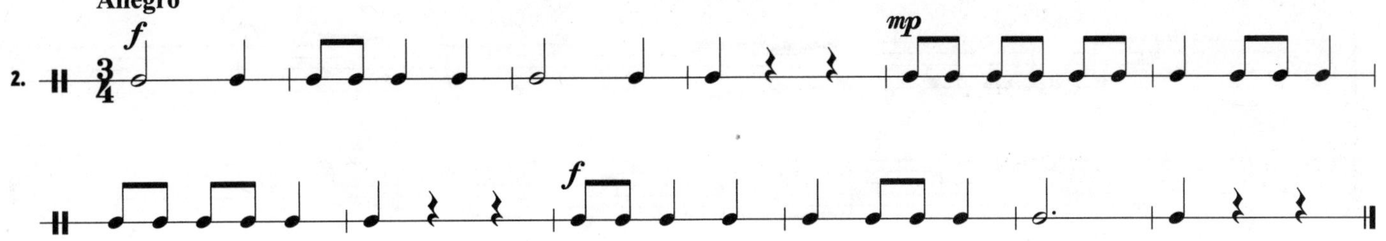

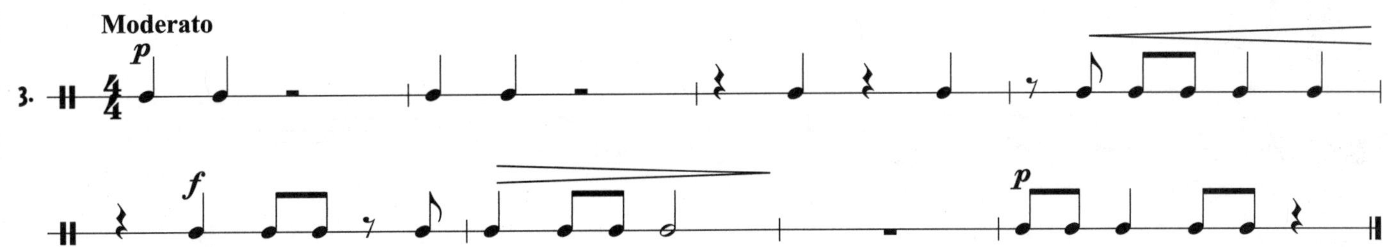

Challenge Exercise

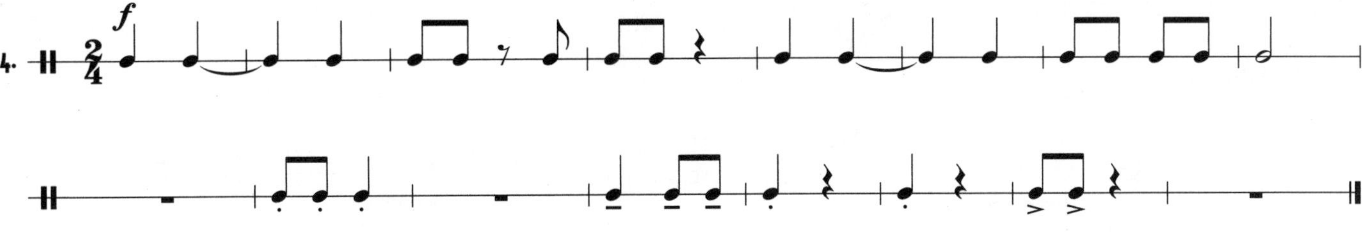

Lesson 1

The following exercises correspond with Lesson 1 in the *Sing at First Sight, Level 2* Textbook and Reproducible Companion.

Hint

It is always helpful to establish a tonal center by singing the tonic triad before sight-singing. In this case, sing *La, Do, Mi, Do, La.*

Challenge Exercise

Lesson 2

The following exercises correspond with Lesson 2 in the *Sing at First Sight, Level 2* Textbook and Reproducible Companion.

1. *mf*

2. **Andante** *mp*

Hint

For the very best crescendo, increase in volume gradually with no sudden changes.

Allegro
4.
mp
mp
Largo
5.
f
f
Challenge Exercise
6.
mf
mf
decresc.
decresc.
p
p

Lesson 3

The following exercises correspond with Lesson 3 in the *Sing at First Sight, Level 2* Textbook and Reproducible Companion.

Hint

Before you sing, look for familiar patterns and intervals.

Andante
4.
mp
cresc.
f
decresc.
p
Challenge Exercise
5.
p
6.
mf
mp
cresc.
f

Lesson 4

The following exercises correspond with Lesson 4 in the *Sing at First Sight, Level 2* Textbook and Reproducible Companion.

1.

Andante
mf
mf
p
p

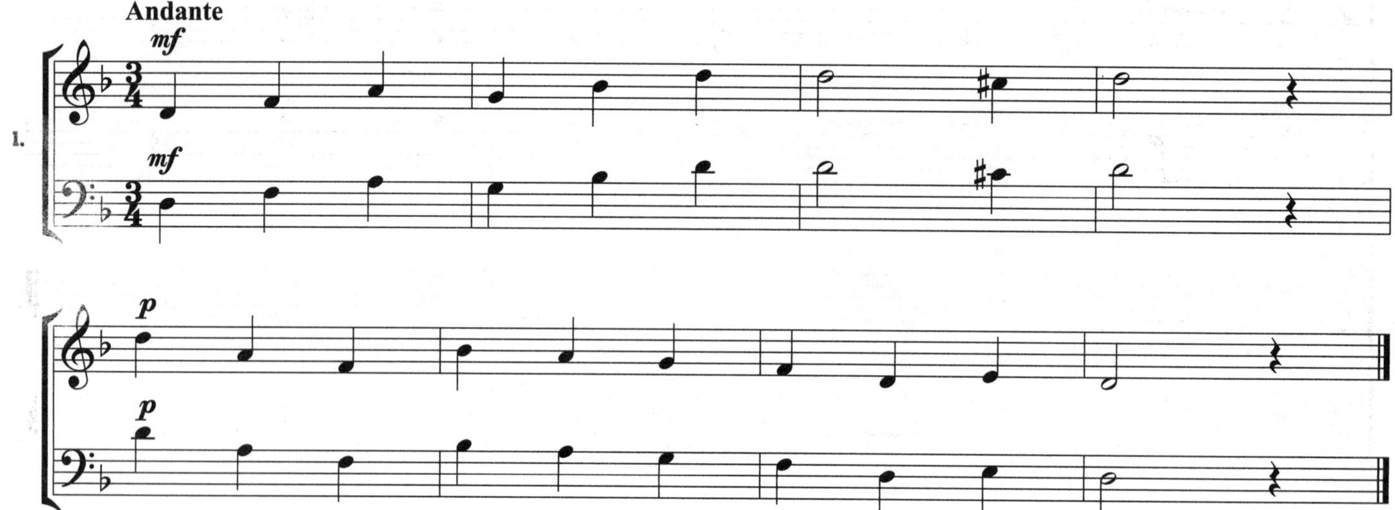

Hint

Practice fast passages slowly at first.

2.

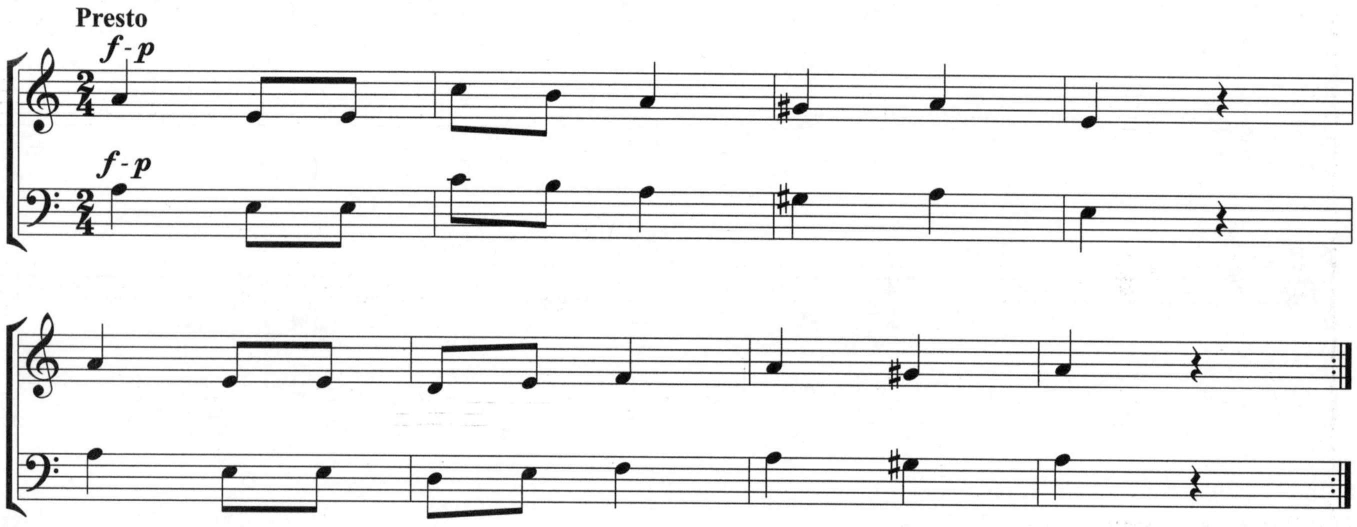
Presto
f - p
f - p

3.

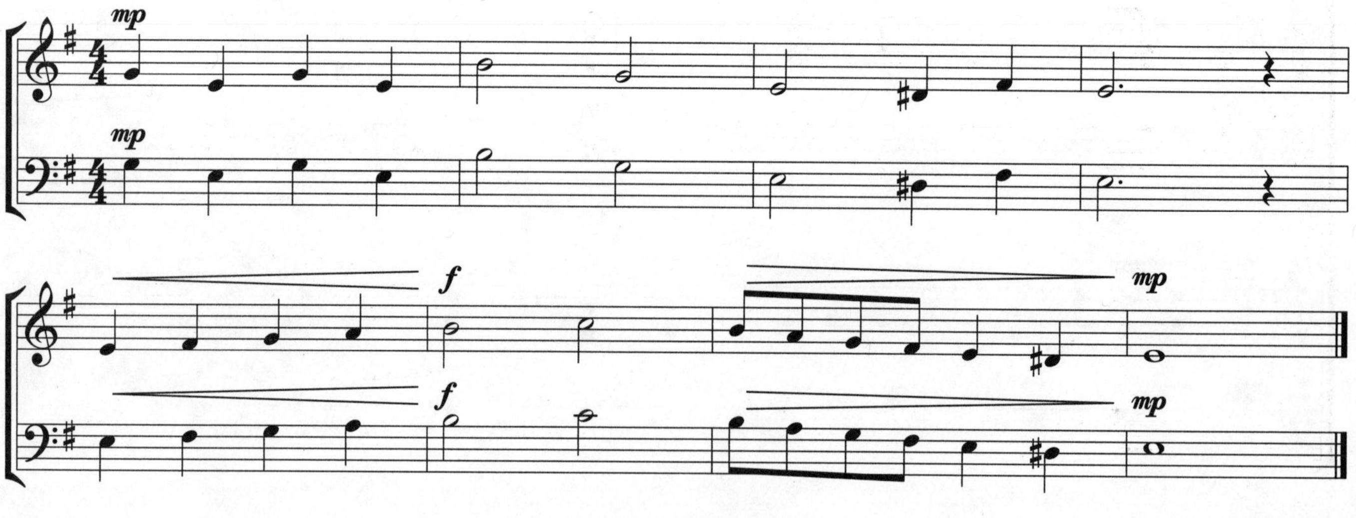
mp
mp
f
mp
f
mp

4.
f
f
Largo
mp
mp
cresc.
cresc.
5.
f
rit.
f
Challenge Exercise
6.
mf
mf
mp
mp
mf
mf
f
f
p
p

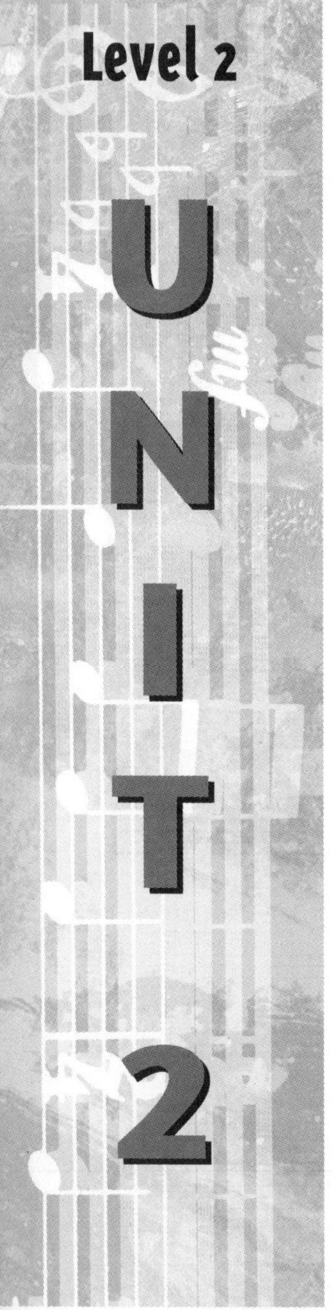

G Minor, B Minor, C Minor, Four-Part Harmony, Di, Ri, Li, Te

Rhythm Readiness 8

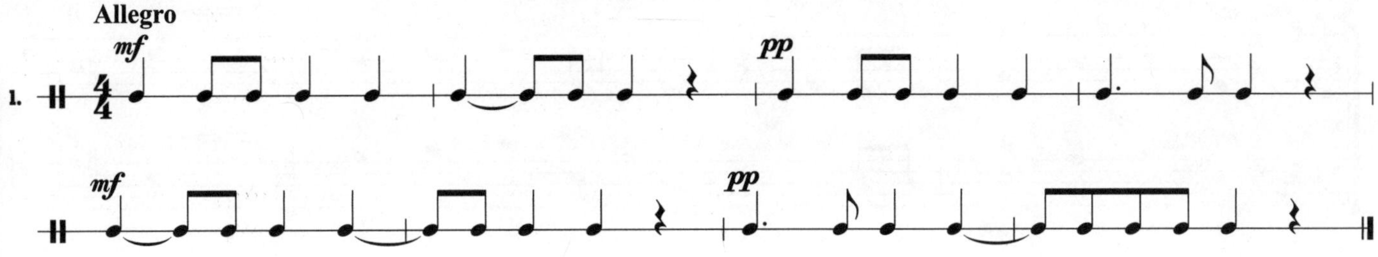
Allegro
mf
1.
pp
mf
pp

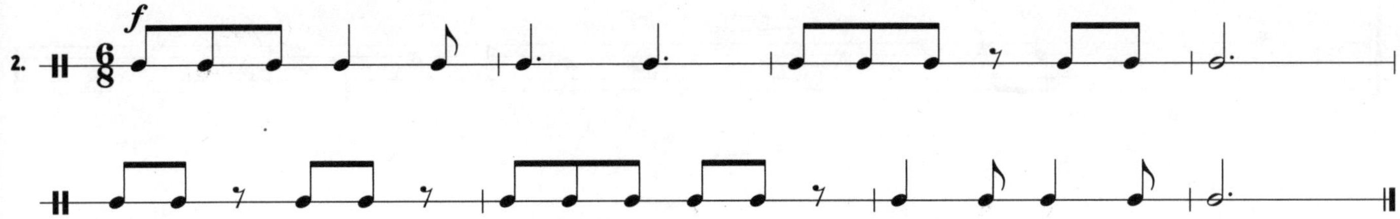
f
2.

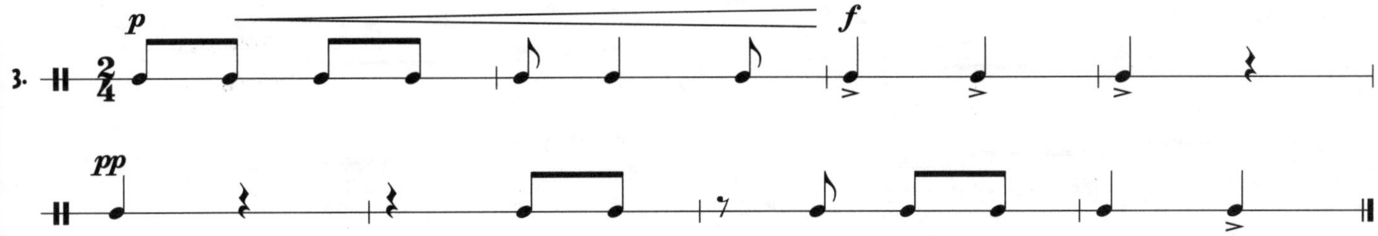
p
f
3.
pp

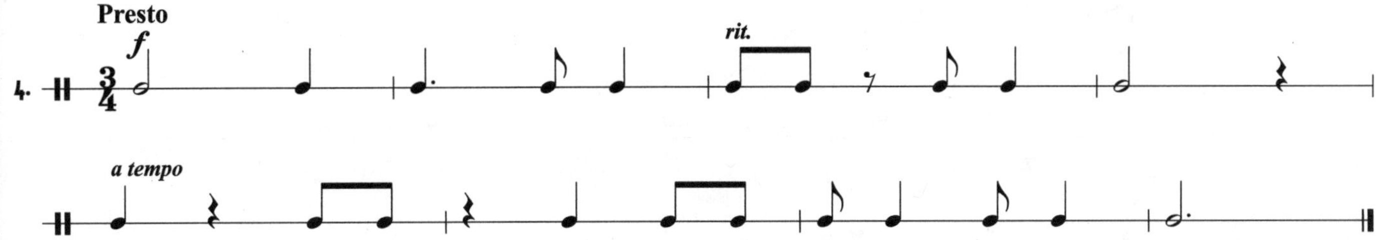
Presto
f
4.
rit.
a tempo

Challenge Exercise

mp
5.

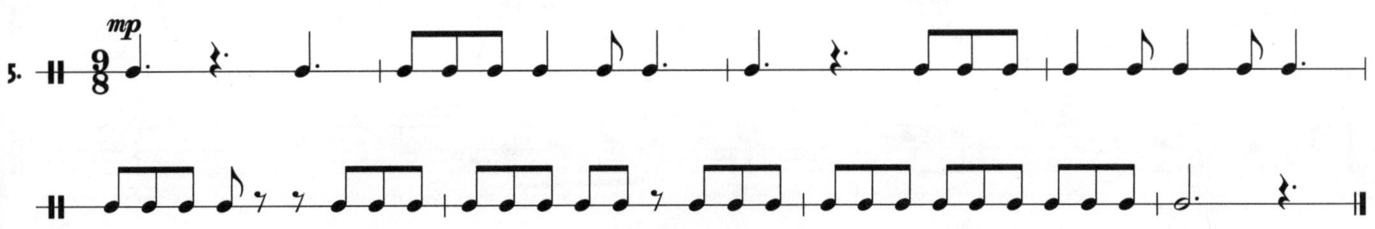

Lesson 5

The following exercises correspond with Lesson 5 in the *Sing at First Sight, Level 2* Textbook and Reproducible Companion.

Allegro

mf

4.

mf

Hint

Many times, it is helpful to tap a dotted quarter note pulse when singing in $\frac{6}{8}$ time.

Challenge Exercise

Lesson 6

The following exercises correspond with Lesson 6 in the *Sing at First Sight, Level 2* Textbook and Reproducible Companion.

Hint

Before singing, identify half steps versus whole steps.

Challenge Exercise

4.

Lesson 7

The following exercises correspond with Lesson 7 in the *Sing at First Sight, Level 2* Textbook and Reproducible Companion.

Challenge Exercise

Presto

4.

f

mp

1.

2. *p* *cresc. poco a poco*

mp

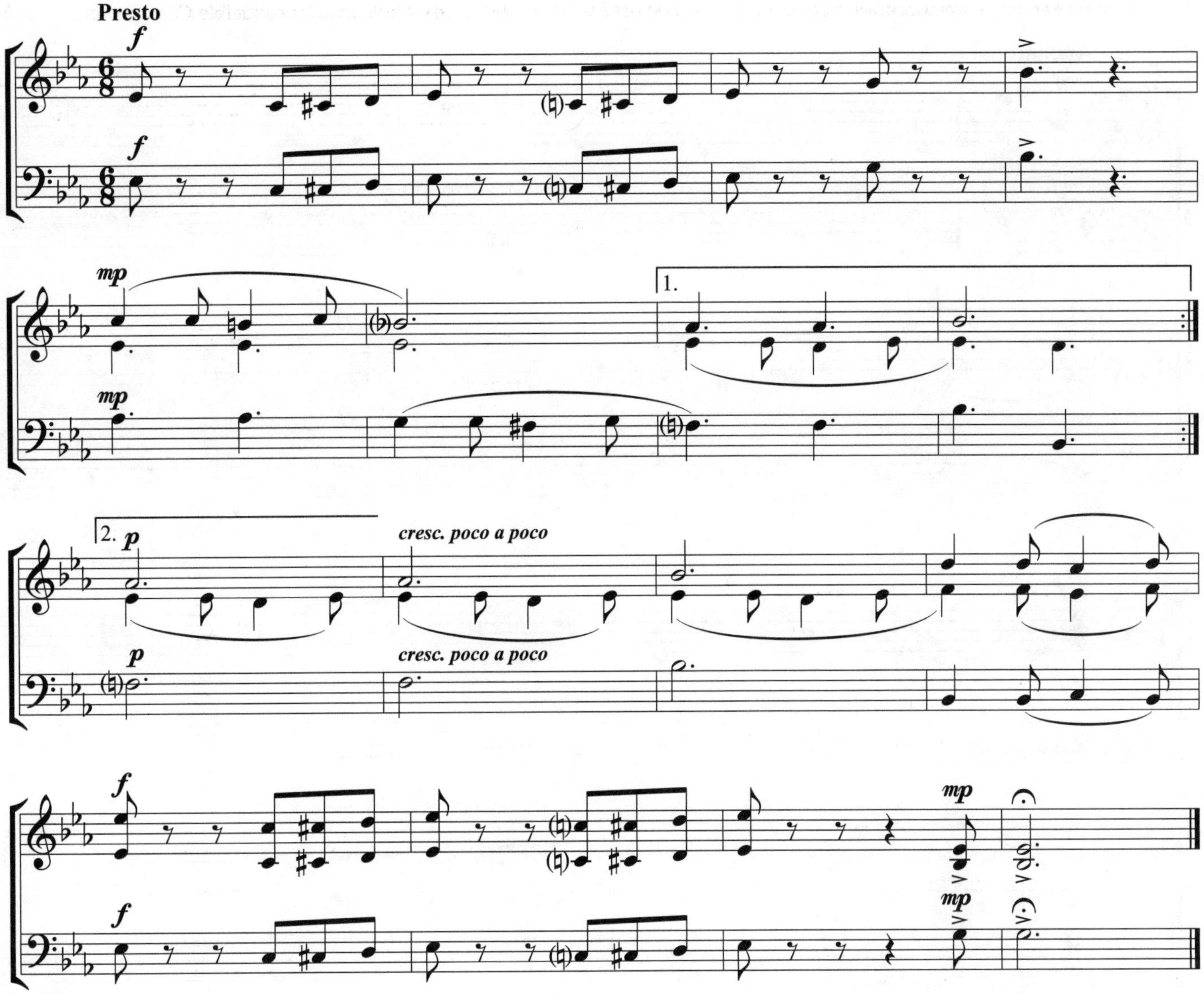

Hint

Note which voice parts work together. Similarities in pitch and rhythm will anchor the ensemble.

Lesson 8

The following exercises correspond with Lesson 8 in the *Sing at First Sight, Level 2* Textbook and Reproducible Companion.

LEVEL 2 • UNIT 2

Hint

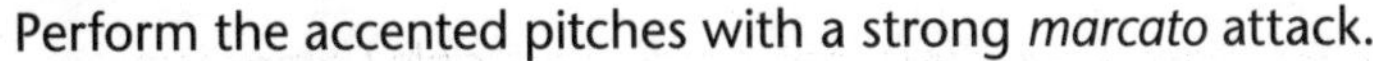

Perform the accented pitches with a strong *marcato* attack.

Challenge Exercise

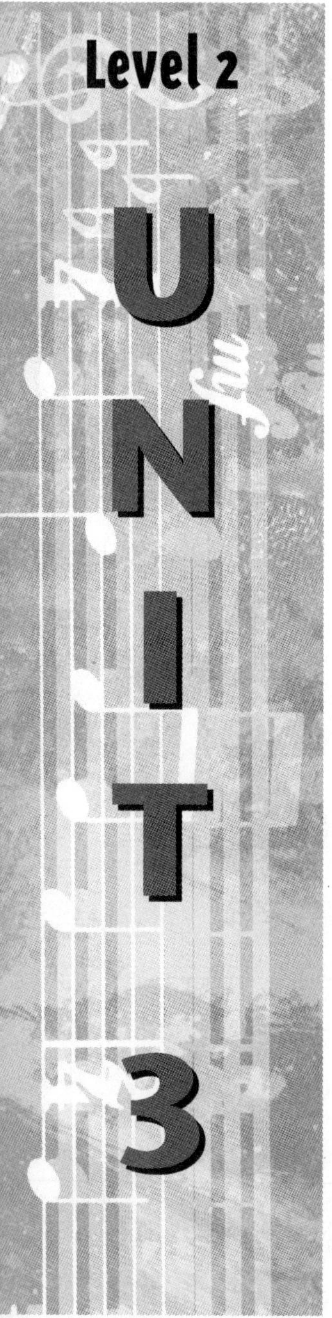

F♯ Minor, F Minor, C♯ Minor, $\frac{5}{4}$ Time, Quarter Note Triplet, Le, Se, Me, Ra

Rhythm Readiness 9

Challenge Exercise

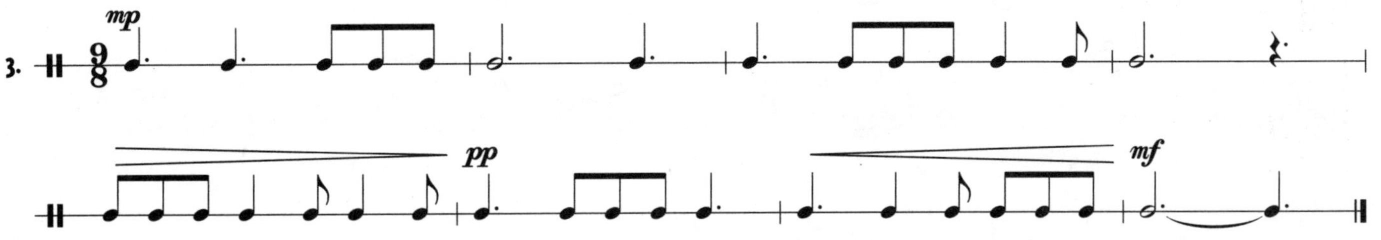

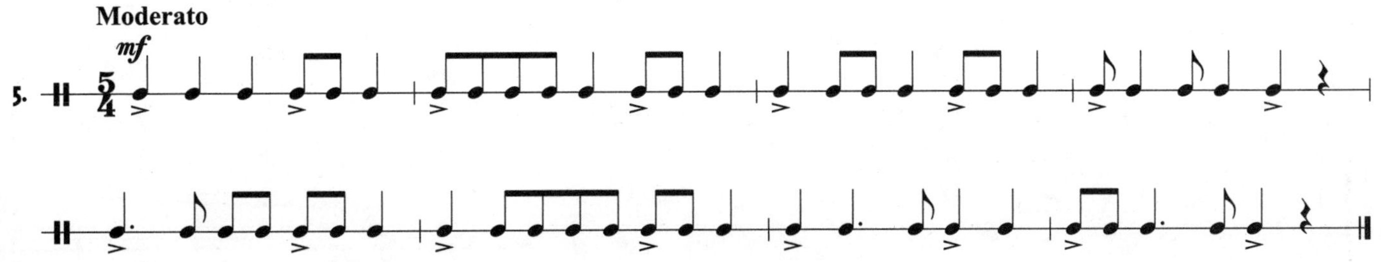

Lesson 9

The following exercises correspond with Lesson 9 in the *Sing at First Sight, Level 2* Textbook and Reproducible Companion.

Andante
4.
p
mp
mf
Challenge Exercise
Moderato
5.
cresc. poco a poco
mf
ff

Lesson 10

The following exercises correspond with Lesson 10 in the *Sing at First Sight, Level 2* Textbook and Reproducible Companion.

When performing long phrases at a slow tempo, stagger breaths to avoid breaks in the choral texture.

Lesson 11

The following exercises correspond with Lesson 11 in the *Sing at First Sight, Level 2* Textbook and Reproducible Companion.

1.

Hint

When performing pick-up notes, determine how many beats are missing from the first measure.

2.

3.

Allegro
f
f
4.
3
Challenge Exercise
mp
mp
5.
mp
mp
cresc.
f
cresc.
f
cresc.
f
cresc.
f

Lesson 12

The following exercises correspond with Lesson 12 in the *Sing at First Sight, Level 2* Textbook and Reproducible Companion.

Challenge Exercise

Hint

A double flat lowers an already flatted pitch by an additional half step. That's one whole step in total.

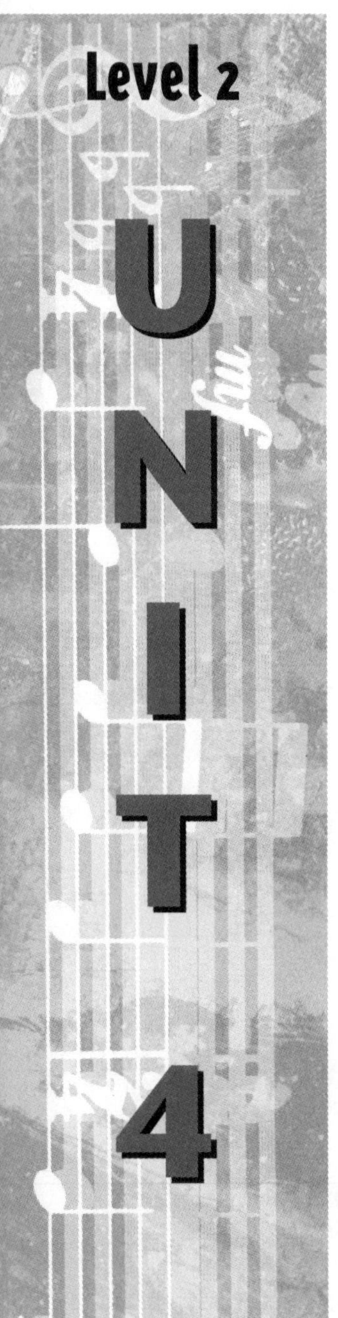

B♭ Minor, G♯ Minor, E♭ Minor, $\frac{12}{8}$ Time, Sixteenth-Eighth-Sixteenth Note Patterns, Chromatic Scale, Major and Minor 2nds, Major and Minor 3rds, 4ths and 5ths (Perfect, Augmented, and Diminished), Major and Minor 6ths and 7ths

Rhythm Readiness 10

Lesson 13

The following exercises correspond with Lesson 13 in the *Sing at First Sight, Level 2* Textbook and Reproducible Companion.

Hint

Hold a fermata for at least double the note's value.

5.

pp

pp

rit.

6.

Adagio

mp

mp

cresc. poco a poco

cresc. poco a poco

f

f

LEVEL 2 • UNIT 4

Lesson 14

The following exercises correspond with Lesson 14 in the *Sing at First Sight, Level 2* Textbook and Reproducible Companion.

Hint

Altering *Mi* to *Me* suggests changing from a major key to a minor key.

Challenge Exercise

LEVEL 2 • UNIT 4

Lesson 15

The following exercises correspond with Lesson 15 in the *Sing at First Sight, Level 2* Textbook and Reproducible Companion.

Challenge Exercise

Hint

When singing tight harmony, be sure to center your own pitch to allow the dissonance to tune.

Lesson 16

The following exercises correspond with Lesson 16 in the *Sing at First Sight, Level 2* Textbook and Reproducible Companion.

Challenge Exercise

Hint

It may be helpful to practice once without the accidentals. This will provide a reference point for larger intervals.

Andante
mf
4.
mf
Allegro
mf
5.
mf
1.
2.
mp
6.
mp
rit.
a tempo

Major and Minor Key Signatures

C Major
(A Minor)

F Major
(D Minor)

G Major
(E Minor)

B♭ Major
(G Minor)

D Major
(B Minor)

E♭ Major
(C Minor)

A Major
(F♯ Minor)

A♭ Major
(F Minor)

E Major
(C♯ Minor)

D♭ Major
(B♭ Minor)

B Major
(G♯ Minor)

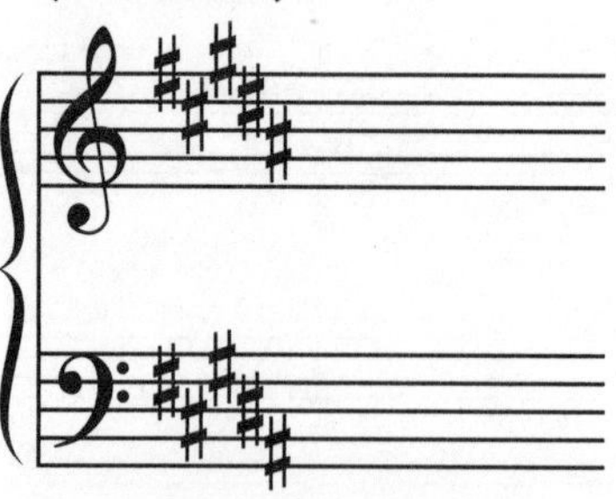

G♭ Major
(E♭ Minor)

Curwen Hand Signs

Flats
♭

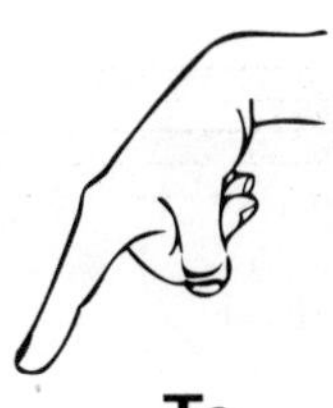

Te

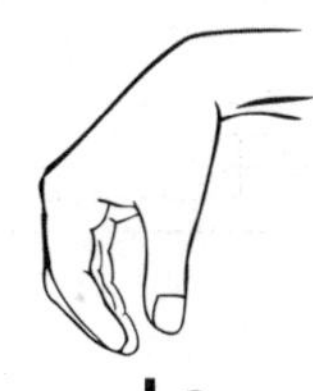

Le

Se

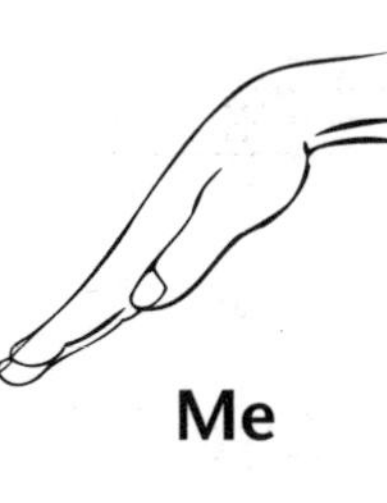

Me

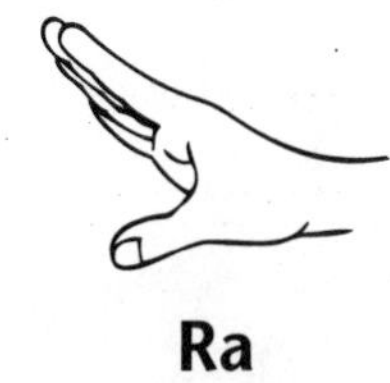

Ra

Do

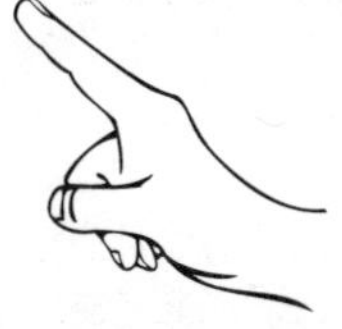

Ti

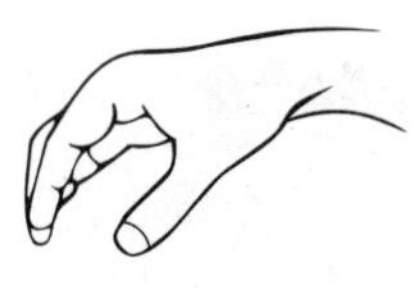

La

Sol

Fa

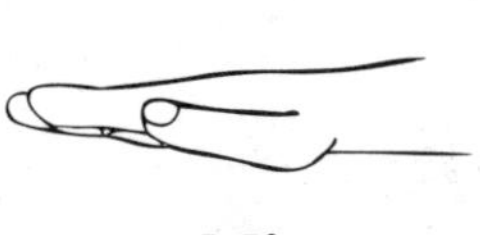

Mi

Re

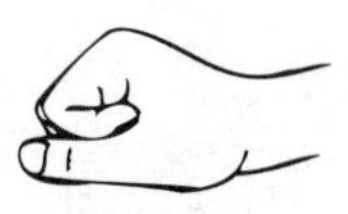

Do

Sharps
♯

Li

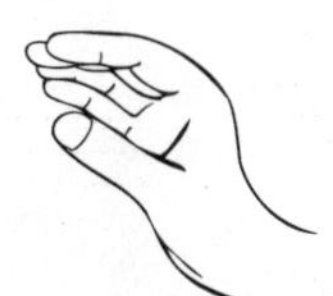

Si

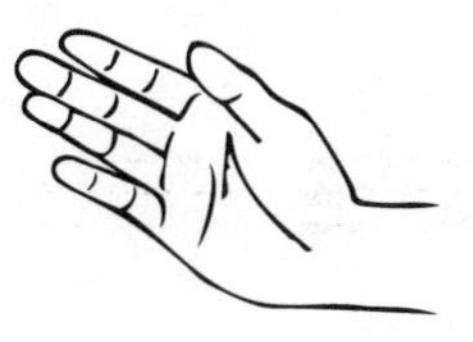

Fi

Ri

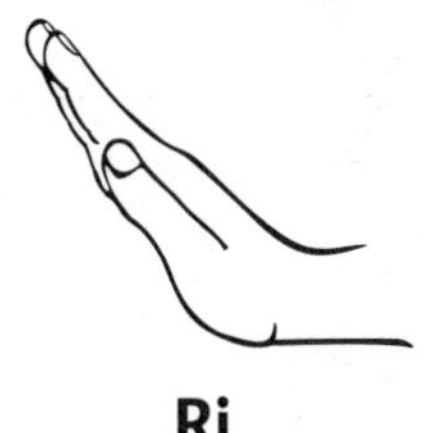

Di

Notes